371·58
Smi

BOOK NO: 264409

KU-214-696

Practical Approaches to Bullying

edited by
Peter K Smith and David Thompson

Caerleon
Library

David Fulton Publishers
London

David Fulton Publishers Ltd
2 Barbon Close, London WC1N 3JX

First published in Great Britain by
David Fulton Publishers 1991

Note: The right of the authors to be identified as the authors of this work has
been asserted by them in accordance with the Copyright, Designs and Patents Act
1988.

Copyright © David Fulton Publishers Ltd

British Library Cataloguing in Publication Data

Practical approaches to bullying
   1. Schools. Bullying.
   I. Smith, Peter K.   II. Thompson, David
   371.58

   ISBN 1-85346-159-8

All rights reserved. No part of this publication may be reproduced, stored in a
retrieval system or transmitted, in any form, or by any means, electronic,
mechanical, photocopying, or otherwise, without the prior permission of the
publishers.

Typeset by Chapterhouse, Formby L37 3PX
Printed in Great Britain by

Printed in Great Britain by BPCC Wheatons Ltd, Exeter

Contents

Contributors

YVETTE AHMAD, Sheffield City Polytechnic

TINY ARORA, North Yorkshire County Council, Scarborough

JOAN BRIER, Wybourn First and Middle School, Sheffield

NORMAN ELLIOTT, Broad Elms School, Sheffield

PAT FOSTER, Thorn Hill High School, Dewsbury, Yorks

FRANCIS GOBEY, Neti-Neti Theatre Company, London

ANGELA M HORTON, University of Exeter

CHRIS HOUSDEN, Bramcote Hills Comprehensive School, Nottingham

CYNTHIA McDOUGALL, HM Prison, Wakefield, Yorkshire

BARRY McGURK, Psychological Services, Farningham, Kent (formerly Home Office Prison Department)

NOTTINGHAMSHIRE EDUCATION COMMITTEE (Peter Foale, Education Officer, Schools), County Hall, West Bridgford

SIMON PRIEST, N. E. Derbyshire Bullying Project, Chesterfield

PETER K. SMITH, University of Sheffield

DAVID THOMPSON, University of Sheffield

DORIS WEST, Salisbury College of Technology, Salisbury, Wilts

IRENE WHITNEY, University of Sheffield

MARTIN WILKINSON, N. E. Derbyshire Bullying Project, Chesterfield

Foreword

No doubt, bullying and victimisation have always been with us. In any social group which it is difficult to leave, it is possible for one or more persons to abuse a position of greater strength or power by systematically hurting another person. This can happen in families, in offices or factories. It is perhaps especially likely in 'closed' institutions such as schools, and also children's homes, detention centres, prisons, the armed services. When bullying and victimisation is exposed, there is generally widespread concern about it. But often, it is difficult to expose; in part, because it is done out of public view; in part, because the victims are often afraid to talk about it; in part, because the authorities may, on occasion, be unwilling to admit there is a problem.

This book is about bullying and victimisation in children and young people, and ways of dealing with it. With the exception of Chapters 12 and 13, it is about bullying in schools. This is a topic which has had extensive media interest recently, and which seemed to reach a peak during 1989–90. The concern is a very understandable one, since most adults will have had some experience of the problem, either as children themselves, or through their own children or their friend's children. Bullying appears to be quite pervasive in schools, and probably to a greater extent than most teachers and parents realise. Yet, coinciding with an increased public awareness is a greater knowledge both of the nature of the problem, and of what can be done about it. This book is intended to play a part in helping teachers, school governors, and parents work towards reducing the effects of behaviour which can, at worst, blight the lives of victims into adulthood and encourage antisocial and violent behaviour in those who get away with bullying.

Peter K. Smith, David Thompson
Sheffield
January 1991

CHAPTER 1

Dealing with Bully/Victim Problems in the U.K.

Peter K. Smith and David Thompson

What is bullying?

Bullying, and related terms such as harassment, can be taken to be a subset of aggressive behaviour. As with aggressive behaviour generally, bullying intentionally causes *hurt* to the recipient. This hurt can be both *physical* or *psychological*; while some bullying takes the form of hitting, pushing, taking money, it can also involve telling nasty stories, or social exclusion. It can be carried out by *one child*, or *a group*.

Three further criteria particularly distinguish bullying. The hurt done is *unprovoked*, at least by any action that would normally be considered a provocation. (Being clumsy, for instance, might invoke some bullying but would not normally be considered a legitimate provocation). Bullying is thought of as a *repeated action*; something that just happens once or twice would not be called bullying. Finally, the child doing the bullying is generally thought of as being *stronger*, or perceived as stronger; at least, the victim is not (or does not feel him/herself to be) in a position to retaliate very effectively. These latter characteristics mean that bullying behaviour can be extremely distressing to the recipient, and the long-term effects particularly unfortunate.

Teasing provides a category of behaviour that overlaps with bullying, being persistently irritating but in a minor way or such that, dependent on context, it may or may not be taken as playful (Pawluk,

1989). In our own work we have included 'nasty teasing' as bullying (see Chapter 10).

Ways of assessing bully/victim problems

There have been several ways of assessing bully/victim problems. Ahmad and Smith (1990) compared a number of different methods on a sample of about 100 children aged 9, 11, 13 and 15 years. One measure used was the 'Life in Schools' booklet of Arora and Thompson (1987). This asks children to report whether a number of kinds of behaviour have happened to them over the last week, as well as asking explicitly about bullying. Children are asked to put their name on the booklet. Another measure was a questionnaire used in Norway by Olweus (1989), modified in slight ways. There is a version for middle school and a slightly more extended version for secondary school, with some 20–25 questions each with multiple-choice answer format. The questionnaire is anonymous and this is stressed when it is administered, usually on a class basis (see Chapter 10).

Thirdly, individual interviews were conducted; these consisted of going through the 'Life in Schools' booklet and the Olweus questionnaire individually with the student, and in addition asking further questions about what bullying is, and if they bullied or were bullied, what happened, and how long did it last. Finally, each class teacher was asked to nominate any bullies or victims in their class, as were children themselves.

We concluded that interviews were not most suitable as a means of studying the *incidence* of bully/victim problems; they did not bring to light new cases, and with some children led to defensive answers. However in the case of students willing to talk about their experiences, they can give a rich insight. Teacher nominations of victims correlated quite well with questionnaire responses, but agreement for bullies was not so high. Peer nominations by children show better agreement and generally show high consistency.

We feel that the best method for establishing incidence from middle school age upwards is the anonymous questionnaire. This can be supplemented by peer nomination for more intensive study of particular groups. Our confidence in the anonymous questionnaire is enhanced by the general consistency children show in answering the 25 or so separate questions. Only a very small proportion of children (around 1 per cent) hand in invalid questionnaires, possibly deliberately. Most treat the exercise very seriously.

The occurrence of bully/victim problems

Using the modified Olweus questionnaire, Yvette Ahmad and Peter Smith estimated the incidence of bully/victim problems in about 2,000 pupils in 7 middle schools and 4 secondary schools in the South Yorkshire area. The questionnaires were given about five to eight weeks into a school term. The results are shown in Table 1.1; figures exclude the responses 'I haven't been bullied', and 'It has only happened once or twice'; and are reported separately for moderate bullying ('sometimes'/'now and then' or more often) and severe bullying ('once a week or more often'). These figures are quite alarming, suggesting an incidence of up to 1 in 5 for being bullied, and up to 1 in 10 for bullying others.

Table 1.1 Approximate percentages of pupils who report being bullied, or bullying other pupils, in four countries. The Norwegian figures are a range based on pre-intervention figures from Roland (1989) and Olweus (1989); the English figures are based on data from Ahmad and Smith; the Irish figures (primary schools only) are from O'Moore and Hillery (1989), and the Scottish figures (secondary schools only) from Mellor (1990). All the studies used a similar questionnaire.

(a) Primary School (approx 7–12 years)	Norway (range)	England (S. Yorkshire)	Ireland (Dublin)
Being bullied 'Sometimes'	7–12	20.1	not reported
Includes 'Once a week or more often'	3–7	6.0	8.0
Bullying others 'Sometimes'	6–8	8.4	not reported
Includes 'Once a week or more often'	2–4	1.7	2.5

(b) Secondary School (approx 13–16 years)	Norway (range)	England (S. Yorkshire)	Scotland (two regions)
Being bullied 'Sometimes'	5–6	17.7	6
Includes 'Once a week or more often'	2–3	7.5	3
Bullying others 'Sometimes'	5–8	10.3	4
Includes 'Once a week or more often'	2–3	3.3	2

There have been earlier reports in England, using different methods of assessment, which have nevertheless come up with figures of the same order of magnitude. These include Lowenstein (1978), J. and E Newson (1984), Kidscape (1986a), Arora and Thompson (1987) and Stephenson and Smith (1989).

Since the questionnaire method used was almost the same as that of Olweus (1989) in his extensive surveys in Norway, we can compare our results directly with his, see Table 1.1. The incidence in middle schools is higher in England, but only for reports of being bullied moderately; the incidence is much more clearly higher in secondary schools. The problem does not seem to decline here in secondary schools in the way in which it does in Norway.

In 1989 there were some press reports that 'Britain is "bullying capital of Europe" ' (*The Guardian*, 28/9/89) and 'Bullying in our schools is worst in Europe – claim' (*Sheffield Star*, 28/9/89). These claims were alarmist, though they did serve to focus concern on what is certainly an unacceptable level of reported bullying. At present however we need a much wider range of data in England, and an examination of urban/rural and regional as well as school differences. There is even less data from other European countries; but some comparable data is included in Table 1.1. Mellor (1990) analysed 942 responses from 10 secondary schools in Scotland, and reported 6 per cent bullied 'sometimes or more often' and 4 per cent bullying 'sometimes or more often'; as low or lower than the Norwegian figures. He states that 'the findings do call into question recent press reports that "Britain is the bullying capital of Europe" '. However a report on 783 children from 4 Dublin primary schools by O'Moore and Hillery (1989), found that 8.0 per cent were seriously bullied (once a week or more often) and 2.5 per cent bullied others this frequently. They conclude that 'these figures indicate an incidence that is about double that in Norway'.

Olweus (1989) surveyed 60 schools in Sweden, and reported that 'bully/victim problems were somewhat greater and more serious in the Swedish schools than the Norwegian schools'. Garcia and Perez (1989) used a questionnaire with 8–12 year olds at 10 schools in Spain. They reported '17.2 per cent bullied this term . . . it is obvious that bullying does take place with nearly a fifth of the school population'. These various findings suggest that Norway (and also Scotland) may have relatively low figures. The figures from Spain and Ireland seem very comparable to those obtained in England.

The nature of bullying

The questionnaire data from these studies also tell us about the nature of bully/victim problems. Most of the children or young people who report being bullied say that it takes the form of teasing; but about a third report other forms such as hitting or kicking, or (more occasionally) extortion of money. These latter may seem the more serious forms, but some 'teasing', especially that related to some disability, or which takes the form of racial or sexual harassment, can be very hurtful.

Racial harassment can be a severe problem in some multi-ethnic schools (Kelly and Cohn, 1988; Burnage Report, 1989). In a study of junior schools in London, Tizard *et al.*, (1988) found that about a third of pupils reported being teased because of their colour; black children more than white children. In a survey by Malik (1990) of 612 secondary school children, again a third reported they had been bullied, and over a third of these reported being bullied by someone from another racial background. A significantly higher proportion of Asian children reported being bullied in this way. Kelly and Cohn (1988) surveyed three secondary schools and found that two-thirds of students reported they had been teased or bullied, and that much of this was name-calling; again Asian children suffered this the most though it was high in all racial groups. The situation in multi-ethnic settings is, however, clearly complex, and variable between particular situations.

There are fairly consistent gender differences. Boys report, and are reported as, bullying more than girls; whereas boys and girls report being bullied, about equally. However there may have been some under-reporting of girls' bullying, as it more usually takes the form of behaviours such as social exclusion, or spreading nasty rumours, rather than the physical behaviours used more by boys. The more physical behaviours are perhaps more obviously seen as bullying, although the psychological forms are also included in our definition (see Chapter 10).

Most of the bullying reported is by children or young people in the same class or at least the same year as the victim. Some is by older pupils, but not surprisingly, little is by younger pupils. Victims are more likely to report being alone at break time, and to feel less well liked at school; having some good friends can be a strong protective factor against being bullied. However this potential support needs to be harnessed; most pupils did not think that peers would be very likely to help stop a child being bullied.

By contrast, many pupils thought that a teacher would try to stop bullying. However despite this general perception, only a minority of victims report that they have talked to a teacher or anyone at home about it, or that a teacher or parent has talked to them about it. Teachers are often not aware of bullying in the playground, since supervision at break time is now undertaken by lunchtime supervisory assistants (who usually receive little if any training for the job). Not all approaches to teachers are sympathetically received, and unless the school has a very definite and effective policy, the bullied child may well feel afraid of retribution for 'telling'. Victims are also often unwilling to involve their parents, partly because they may blame themselves, partly because of embarrassment and possible unforeseen consequences if the parents go to complain to the school.

Possible subgroups of children who are bullied or victimised

Although it is tempting to talk of 'bullies' and 'victims', it is possible and indeed likely that this is an over-simple typology. Using data based mainly on teacher reports, Stephenson and Smith (1989) suggested five main types of children are involved. 'Bullies' are strong, assertive, easily provoked, enjoy aggression, and have average popularity and security. 'Anxious bullies' by contrast have poor school attainment, and are insecure and less popular. 'Victims' tend to be weaker, lack self-confidence, and are less popular with peers. 'Provocative victims' by contrast are active, stronger, easily provoked, and often complain about being picked on. Finally, 'bully/victims' are also stronger and assertive, and are amongst the least popular children, both bullying others and complaining about being victimised.

Olweus (1978) distinguished between 'passive' victims (anxious, insecure, failed to defend themselves) and 'provocative' victims (hot-tempered, created tension, fought back), and Perry, Kusel and Perry (1988) made a similar distinction between low-aggressive and high-aggressive victims. These provisional typologies need further investigation. It is also worth bearing in mind that some people object to the terms 'bully' and 'victim' as having dangerous possibilities in labelling children in undesirable ways. At least so far as discussing specific children is concerned, it may be better to talk only of 'bullying behaviour' rather than of 'bullies' per se.

Consequences of being bullied, or bullying others

How much does bullying really matter? One can still encounter the view that bullying is a training for 'real life' and a necessary part of growing up. Yet the more serious forms of bullying, at least, can have very serious consequences; 'real life' would no doubt seem a welcome escape for those being victimised. For children being bullied, their lives are being made miserable often for some considerable period of time. Already probably lacking close friends at school, they are likely to lose confidence and self-esteem even further. The peer rejection which victims often experience is a strong predictor of later adult disturbance (Parker and Asher, 1987). Research by Gilmartin (1987), using retrospective data, found that some 80 per cent of 'love-shy' men (who despite being heterosexual found it very difficult to have relationships with the opposite sex) had experienced bullying or harassment at school.

We are not yet certain whether bullying in itself may cause such later relationship problems; but some insight can be obtained from in-depth life history interviews. The following extract, obtained from a woman aged 28 who experienced being bullied through much of her school career, and was just engaged to be married, illustrates how intense bullying in the middle school period seems to have left a long-term anxiety about children which, while not precluding a heterosexual relationship, is having an impact:

> *Do you feel that's left a residue with you . . . what do you feel the effects are?*
> . . . I'm quite insecure, even now . . . I won't believe that people like me . . . and also I'm frightened of children . . . and this is a problem. He [fiance] would like a family, I would not and I don't want a family because I'm frightened of children and suppose they don't like me?
> . . . those are things that have stayed with me. It's a very unreasonable fear but it is there and it's very real.

The most severe consequences of bullying, thankfully rare but not unknown, can be the actual suicide of the victim, or their death as a direct or indirect result of bullying, as in the Burnage High School case (Burnage Report, 1989).

There are also consequences for those who bully others, with impunity. They are learning that power-assertive and sometimes violent behaviour can be used to get their own way. Unless counteracted, such forms of behaviour can have considerable continuity over time (Olweus, 1979; Lane, 1989), and lead to further undesirable outcomes. A follow-up by Olweus (1989) in Norway, of secondary school pupils to age 24, found that former school bullies were nearly four times more likely than non-bullies to have had three or more court convictions. In the UK, Lane (1989) reports that involvement in bullying at school is a strong predictor of delinquency; though the overall level of delinquency is higher in boys, the association with earlier bullying is in fact stronger for girls.

Factors influencing the extent of bullying behaviour

Many factors are likely to be implicated in the occurrence and extent of bullying behaviour; what follows is a brief summary of some of the more important, categorised as child, family, school and societal factors.

Starting with child characteristics, temperament is one obvious consideration. Children differ in temperament very soon after birth, and these characteristics show some stability. This may relate to the impulsiveness and quick-tempered response of bullying children, or the withdrawal and lack of assertiveness of victims.

Another characteristic of children is the extent to which they are socially competent or socially skilled in situations of conflict, frustration or ambiguity. Do children who get involved in bullying or being bullied, lack social skills? Dodge *et al.*, (1986) describe social competence in children as a five-stage processing model: encoding the stimulus situation/interpreting it/search for suitable responses/evaluating the best response/enacting the chosen response. Thus, any 'deficit' in social competence would be ascribed to one or more of these stages. The research in the U.S. has largely been on high aggressive children, and there is some evidence that such children tend to interpret ambiguous situations as hostile (i.e. more readily attributing hostile intentions to others), and to generate fewer non-hostile responses (Dodge and Frame, 1982; Guerra and Slaby, 1989). However the evidence is far from consistent.

Children who bully others may be less empathic to the feelings of others, such as potential victims. Certainly both the typical responses they make, to questionnaires and to interviews, suggest that they tend to feel positive or neutral about seeing bullying incidents, whereas most children say they feel bad or unhappy about them. Yet another view is that some children who bully others, rather than lacking social skills, simply have different values, and goals for social encounters (Smith & Boulton, 1990). Interviews with bullies often suggest that they view the playground as a tough place where you need to dominate or humiliate others in order not to be so treated yourself.

What about the characteristics of victims? Rather less information is available about the social skills of children who get victimised. Still, the view that they have a 'deficit' in social skills may be more plausible for victims than for bullies. Many (though not all) victims are sociometrically rejected (e.g. Perry *et al.*, 1988), and questionnaire responses show that victims feel they lack friends and peer support in the playground.

Victims may also be distinguished by some physical characteristic such as clumsiness, obesity, disability, or hair colour different from the majority. Olweus (1989) failed to find such associations in his Norwegian studies; he did however use a very wide range of defining physical characteristics, which may have made his test for this association less sensitive. Stephenson and Smith (1989) did find evidence for this in the UK, from teacher reports. We saw earlier how skin colour can also be associated with bullying.

Family factors have often been implicated, and most clearly by the Norwegian research (Olweus, 1989). For children who bully others, associations are found with cold rather than warm child rearing, high levels of discord or violence in the home, and a lack of clear rules about discipline, or monitoring of behaviour. This is borne out for high aggressive children by research in the U.S. (Patterson *et al.*, 1989). Children growing up in such families are having bullying behaviour modelled for them, with little countervailing affectional or monitoring constraint.

The incidence of bully/victim problems can vary very considerably between individual schools, as research both here and in Scandinavia has shown. Child/family factors will account for part of this, but it is very likely that school ethos is an important factor in social behaviour, as it is for academic attainment (Rutter *et al.*, 1979). There are a number of ways to improve the schools' response to bullying, many discussed in this book. These include having an explicit policy on bullying (Chapters 2, 11, 14); using appropriate non-violent procedures (Chapters 2, 5); involving children themselves, for example through 'bully courts' (Chapter 3); dealing with the issues in the curricular framework, for example using drama and stories (Chapters 6 to 8); working with individual children who bully others (Pikas, 1989), or who are victims (Chapter 4); and improving the quality and supervision of playground time (Blatchford, 1989).

Finally, the role of the wider community and society is undoubtedly important. The apparently differing extents of bullying problems in Britain and in Scandinavia, may reflect in part a wider difference in societal attitudes to violence; the latter countries have pioneered legislation against physical punishment and smacking of children, even by parents. It may also reflect the extent of social class differentiation persisting in the two countries. The level of socio-economic stress on families, the amount of violence shown on the mass media, and the levels of violence, racial and sexual harassment in a society generally, will also be important factors in historical and cultural variation.

Intervention strategies in schools

A lot can be done to reduce bully/victim problems in schools, and there is now considerable evidence that interventions can be effective. The most extensive intervention has been carried out in Norway. Research in Scandinavia in the 1970's had already shown how widespread the problem was. National concern in Norway peaked following one week in 1982 when two children separately committed suicide because of bullying. A nationwide intervention campaign was started, with the backing of the Ministry of Education, in 1983. A resource pack, consisting of a videotape for class discussion, a booklet for teachers, and a folder of advice for parents, was provided for (and to varying extents used by) every middle and secondary school in the country.

There have been two documented follow-up assessments of the effects of this intervention. One was carried out by Erling Roland and Elaine Munthe (Roland, 1989; Munthe, 1989) near Stavanger. Their reports so far analyse results from 37 schools over the period 1983–86. They found an increase in bullying over this period, but less so (with a slight decrease) in schools which used the resource pack most thoroughly. Thus, this finding seems to suggest that the problem may be getting worse on a societal basis (or possibly some non-equivalence in the testing situations at the different time points, may have contributed to the overall time change results). But the resource pack and intervention, when used appropriately, did have an effect.

The second analysis is by Dan Olweus (1989) in the Bergen area, on 42 schools. It uses a cohort-sequential design, starting with 11–14 year olds in 1983, and using exactly the same testing procedures at three time points (1983/84/85). This design enables comparisons of same-age children who have, or have not, experienced the intervention to various extents. The results show a clear and marked decrease (for both boys and girls) in reports of being bullied, bullying others, and of antisocial behaviour generally; and an increase in reported liking of school. The effects on self-reported bullying are supported by data from peer nominations. The effect size is of the order of 50 per cent. This important finding suggests that a properly funded national intervention campaign can have a marked and successful impact.

Other countries, notably the USA and Japan, are developing programmes about bullying in schools. The recent volume edited by Roland and Munthe (1989) has contributions from Holland, Ireland, Italy, Portugal, and Spain, as well as the U.K.

Recent action in the U.K.

In 1989/90 there was a marked upsurge of public interest in the topic of bullying and victimisation in schools, accompanied by intensive media publicity. In 1989 three books on the topic appeared: D. Tattum and D. Lane (eds), *Bullying in Schools*; E. Roland and E. Munthe (eds), *Bullying: An International Perspective*; and V. Besag, *Bullies and Victims in Schools*.

The Elton Report (1989) on discipline in schools, although primarily on teacher-pupil relations and discipline, did mention problems of bullying in a few paragraphs. It stated that

> Recent studies of bullying in schools suggest that the problem is widespread and tends to be ignored by teachers . . . Research suggests that bullying not only causes considerable suffering to individual pupils but also has a damaging effect on school atmosphere . . .
> **We therefore recommend that headteachers and staff should: be alert to signs of bullying and racial harassment; deal firmly with all such behaviour; and take action based on clear rules which are backed by appropriate sanctions and systems to protect and support victims.**
> (op. cit, pp. 102–103).

Based on this report and the widespread concern about the issue, the DES is funding a study in Sheffield from 1991–93 which will assist 20 schools in their intervention policies, monitor their implementation, and assess their effectiveness. The results will be disseminated on a national basis.

The Gulbenkian Foundation set up an advisory working group on 'Bullying in schools' from 1989–90. This has funded several initiatives. One is a 32-page booklet, *Bullying: A positive response* by Delwyn

Tattum and Graham Herbert (1990), available at nominal cost (£1.25); it contains basic information on the nature of the problem, personal experiences, suggestions for coping, and useful addresses and sources for further information. With the launch of this booklet the Gulbenkian Foundation also supported a 3-month extension of the Childline telephone service to a special Bullying Line which received some 40–200 calls a day. It has also supported the development of a survey service for schools, described further in Chapter 10. The Gulbenkian Foundation has also funded materials for Kidscape, presentations by the Neti-Neti Theatre Company (see Chapter 7), and for the preparation of an annotated bibliography and resource guide on anti-bullying materials and strategies during 1991.

The Kidscape organisation in London, directed by Michele Elliott, has produced materials specifically on bullying. It has particularly directed attention to role-playing techniques, and to 'bully courts' in which a children's court would arbitrate on bullying incidents (Kidscape, 1986b; Elliott, 1991).

Case studies have been reported of anti-bullying policies and curricula in individual schools (Arora, 1989; Herbert, 1989; and several chapters in this book). Cooperative group work can lead pupils to work together for a common goal, and can give an opportunity for open discussion of difficulties in interpersonal behaviour. Such techniques, also used by Herbert (1989) in a secondary school, and forming a component of the Norwegian intervention, may well have an important part to play in developing appropriate curricular materials (Cowie and Rudduck, 1988, 1991).

In conclusion, we know that bullying in schools is widespread. The consequences, both for children who are victimised, and for children who bully others, can be severe and sometimes long-lasting. We also know that intervention strategies can be developed, and we have good evidence that they can be effective. Given this knowledge, we have a moral obligation to act on it; put simply, we know that unnecessary suffering can be avoided. A considerable amount of work is now underway in the UK and we can reasonably hope that over the next few years the scale of this problem can be considerably reduced.

Acknowledgements

We are grateful to the ESRC (Swindon) and the Gulbenkian Foundation (London) for their financial support.

CHAPTER 2

Bullying: Towards a Non-Violent Sanctions Policy

Pat Foster and David Thompson

When bullying becomes an issue in school, either because of a few incidents recognised by the staff, because of a school's efforts to reassure parents that all is well, because of a survey, or during the development of a whole school policy on disciplinary matters, the natural temptation is to use the same form of disciplinary sanctions against a child found bullying as in other situations needing disciplinary action. But this is problematic in the specific instance of bullying, because the bully accepts aggression as a central part in his or her understanding of the world.

If disciplinary action is to be truly effective, sanctions have to emerge from social peer pressure on the bully and be accepted by the bully as appropriate, and should not involve explicit aggression on the part of adults. The action has to be consistent with the efforts of school staff to establish a social climate where physical aggression is not used as a means of gaining popularity, maintaining group leadership, or influencing others to do what they are told. The sanctions against bullying have to emerge from the views of the children involved themselves, supported by the adults. This is easier said than done, and this chapter describes the attempts of one secondary school to work towards a social climate where bullying is recognised as unacceptable throughout the school, amongst both children and adults, and where sanctions come from group work with the children concerned.

Is there a problem?

Even this question can only be properly considered in a school where staff have asked themselves specific questions about 'How do we value children?'. All teachers everywhere would think that they do positively value children, but to make the question 'Do we have a problem with bullying?' meaningful, staff need to have set a tone and an atmosphere for valuing children and to have set particular goals which are the practical expression of these general background attitudes. This clearly is a task which needs support from the senior management team, and would be very difficult to achieve unless a clear majority of that team had these aims as priority areas for the school development programme. Even building up this actively positive attitude to children would need an in-service staff education and training programme over perhaps a term, involving departmental heads in the curriculum aspects and more specific training with form tutors and year heads. Such a programme would be very unlikely to 'convert' everybody, but most people in school would be becoming aware of the direction of change and would have heightened awareness of the implications of their own experiences in the classroom and the corridors.

This development process can be greatly helped by involving outside agencies as catalysts, to present a view of the children's experiences and the school's activities which are seen from a different perspective. Educational psychologists, education social workers, and behavioural support teachers often develop different experiences of children and it can be a shock when an education social worker comes in and says that this child feels that Mr. or Mrs. Smith is not on their side, or that the school doesn't care about what happens to them. To get these home truths told to the school it is very important to use other people to help you.

Even when the school felt it did actively value children, many staff did not feel that bullying was a problem for our children in our school. Admitting or accepting that there is a 'problem' of bullying in school can be painful, and this difficulty is compounded if staff are uncertain what, if anything, can be done about it. Our first surveys, done with the help of the school psychologist, were really undertaken to find out if there was a problem. They showed there was cause for concern, and the evidence from the surveys and from case studies of particular incidents in school did go a long way towards convincing people that there needed to be a change. Many teachers see the academic achievement of children as being very important, and these surveys also helped to point out to staff that if a child is very upset about bullying then they are not going to learn very effectively in the classroom. Staff will go along with changes in practices and procedures when they see the link between children being involved in threatening and aggressive situations, or bullying, and the academic achievements of those children. A sense of threat and anxiety is not helpful in establishing good motivation for learning.

What did the parents think?

Valuing children and doing the bullying surveys were developments that were welcomed by parents. Parents are very concerned about bullying, especially when their 11 or 12 year old is just starting in the secondary school. One of the reasons behind our initial survey work to establish the extent of bullying in school was to meet the concerns which parents expressed. We recognised that concern and even encouraged them to talk about it. This discussion began when they first made contact with the school in the summer term before their child started with us. If schools wish parents to be directly involved in encouraging children to behave cooperatively in school, it must be made clear to them right from the beginning that their involvement is welcomed and that we are prepared to take their questioning and their concerns seriously.

Every year, when we have our parent's evening for new parents, we organise the discussion in groups of six parents with one member of staff and one member of our school support services, such as an educational psychologist or an educational social worker. If we have any probationary teachers that year, we may well include one of them as a third member of staff, so that they can learn something of methods of talking to parents in a more open situation than the traditional five or ten minutes of individual discussion, which mainly focuses on the level of children's work.

In the group discussions, we encourage parents to talk about their anxieties and their dilemmas in their children's schooling, and we put some common issues on the agenda by having prompt cards, which describe situations that parents commonly encounter during their children's schooling. We ask them, 'How would you respond to that?'. One card might say, 'Your child has come home from school and says they are being picked on by a pupil or a teacher'. A second one might be, 'Your child says that they do not want to go to school in the mornings, when you are fairly sure they are not physically ill, and the child refuses to tell you why'. We tell the parents, 'What may be small in your eyes as an adult may not be small for your son or daughter. For them it may be an enormous worry. Please come into school and tell us, because it may be something that in year 1 we can put right'. When they do come in to express their concerns they fairly often say 'Well you might think this is silly and I do, but you said I had to come and tell you about any concerns that we noticed'.

These parents' evenings do take a little organisation. All members of staff are involved and they have all had the situation cards so they actually know how to start the discussion. The school support staff have also had the situation cards. The school has to commit itself to use part of the directed time, so all staff feel happy about staying for the full evening. The first year that this was done, we specifically trained the staff by getting them together to discuss a general school view on issues likely to be raised. During the small group discussions with parents, bullying is treated as one issue of concern both to school and to parents; their involvement in limiting it is sought just as their involvement is sought in other aspects of school life, for example attendance and other disciplinary matters. We talk about it being a partnership and a contract, and say explicitly that we have a certain accountability to the parents, and they they too have an accountability in terms of making sure that they support what we would recommend as far as the children are concerned. To tackle bullying effectively in a secondary school there is a need to talk honestly to the parents about some of the anxieties they are going to have to face. When specific incidents of bullying do occur, we always involve the parents of both the bullies and the victims in the school's response to the incident, and we see these group discussions with parents as preparing them for that involvement.

Developing a supportive social climate through the curriculum

There are two slightly different ways of seeing this task. One is to consider the actual curriculum in the various timetabled areas such as English, Humanities, Personal and Social Education, and the ways in which the content and activities of teaching in these areas can help to develop supportive social relationships. The second perspective is to consider the opportunities for any group work which may occur across the full range of activities in school, which would include ad hoc arrangements such as assemblies on specific topics, special joint meetings with junior school children, meetings about particular incidents of bullying which need discussion by the children, and indeed any forum which helps children to develop and express their own individual and corporate views about bullying and related issues. In practice, of course, these two perspectives have a large area of overlap, in that much teaching in many timetabled subject areas involves group work with varying degrees of structure and student-centred content (Cowie and Rudduck, 1988, 1991).

Looking first at the use of timetabled subject areas, the obvious one is personal, social and health education. It is important to have developed general discussions of an appropriate PSHE curriculum across all the staff involved in teaching it. In this way issues concerned with bullying and aggression can be brought directly to all the children in the school. Bullying and the school's appropriate response to it are very much emphasised in our first year, in the first term, but it is also cyclical in that it is actually returned to in the curriculum in the second, third, fourth and fifth years. This gives a very direct context with the tutor and the pupils, which can address the nitty gritty about what to do in certain situations. Very often drama is used, since when the children see something happening visually and take part in it, it has a greater impact. The staff have developed appropriate materials to use in the PSHE curriculum, so that all staff members have some support in classroom routines to address these issues.

The curriculum dimension goes further than PSHE alone. For example, in the first year for about twenty five per cent of the time the students would be having lessons with one person, constituting a foundation programme, concerned with raising awareness of the issues of conflict and conflict resolution within a particular institution but also nationally and in a world sense. We called it a global education programme and based it on work some staff had done whilst completing the York University Diploma in Global and Multicultural Education. Clearly there have to be ways of cross-curricular mapping when considering the coordination of topics raised in different subject areas, so we produced a skill matrix of the first year and the second year curriculum, to identify in which subject areas particular knowledge and skills were included. We also included social skills in this matrix. We found it a useful exercise to do because it showed not only when particular knowledge and skills were being reinforced by different subject teaching, but also where there was too much duplication both inside subject areas and between them.

One example outside the usual curriculum involved inviting children from the junior school to come to the secondary school in the July before they were due to join us; rather than have a staff-directed visit, we used group work. We stopped the timetable for our existing first year for two complete afternoons, and set up groups of roughly six children of whom four were from the junior schools and two were from our own first year. The content of this group work was structured through encouraging our existing first year students to produce an alternative prospectus, during PSHE lessons, for the children at the upper end of the junior schools, talking about who the significant people were in the secondary school, what happened in school, how the various school procedures operated. We intended to have a 'problem page' in the alternative prospectus as well as a detailing of some of the nice things. When the prospectus was produced, by the first year children, it was then used as a basis for the discussion groups with the children from the junior schools.

We had been careful to structure the groups so that the children from the junior school coming in would be able to say all they wanted to, by only having two of our first years with a group of four junior school students. We split each of our first year classes in two, and half the class went and did some work in the library while the other half were the hosts for the visitors. On the second afternoon the groups were reversed so that all our first years were involved. Comments from the junior school staff and from the parents of the children when we met them at our parents' evening seemed to indicate that the experience had been very successful.

In such ways, both through subject-based work and taking general opportunities for group work in the school, a school ethos can be established where all children, including the 'silent majority' who were hardly ever themselves directly involved with bullying either as a bully or a victim, can be encouraged to adopt an attitude of non-toleration of bullying behaviour. Just because the bully usually takes care to avoid his or her activities being easily identified by responsible adults, the establishment of these social standards of what is and is not acceptable among the average students is crucial for the success of an anti-bullying policy.

Using school structures to demonstrate support for individual students

One of the major features of victims of bullying is a tendency to lack self-confidence and self-esteem. This view was supported by our survey of children's views on bullying, when we noticed that some of the children who tended to report more incidents of bullying were also children that we knew were under-achieving.

In order to establish a school climate in which as many pupils as possible are confident and have good self-esteem, a school has to recognize other criteria for approval apart from the usual academic and sporting ones. To move towards this goal, our school changed from banding to a mixed ability teaching system. This prevented the obvious dominance of academic achievement. We felt that if such dominance was reflected in the major social structure of the school then it would be difficult to value such aspects of the children as their personalities and non-academic achievements.

We also decided that we would find some other way of rewarding and approving of children which had nothing to do with academic achievement so we began a merit system. There were no de-merits, and the merits could be awarded for almost anything, from making an effort to get to school on time in spite of difficulties due to family commitments, through to establishing a creative arts week in the lower school involving painting, singing, drama, pottery, and games. In the latter, children took part either as class groups or as individuals; the idea was that all children should be encouraged to applaud and appreciate what the other members of their class were doing even if it was not a highly sophisticated performance. These weeks happened once in the summer and once in the winter, for the first and second years in school. Lessons were cancelled during this period, and children were doing things that interested them and were off the normal curriculum, showing some of their skills and qualities that they were not able to show in the normal institutionalized pattern of school life. Almost more importantly, the rest of the children actually recognized and applauded them for doing that.

Children's achievements are supported in another way by the requirement that staff assessing work must always write some positive comment on the work. Even the observation that a child has not spent enough time on the task must be put in a positive way. We amended the report and recording practices and have moved to a record of achievement model. Although the staff have to approve of the children's self-assessment this model does in fact raise their self-esteem. This is because tutors are sitting down with each child and saying 'Let's list the positive things that you have done'. The child then writes a paragraph summarizing their achievements. We are also planning to include these records on the computer system so that by the end of a year the children will have accumulated a number of A4 sheets on their own achievements.

Another area where we tried to encourage self-confidence and self-esteem amongst as wide a number of children as possible was to move from an orthodox prefect system to one where children volunteered to be prefects. The staff carefully looked at the volunteers in terms of building up teams and with specific areas of responsibility for the individuals in each team.

A further way that general school routines and procedures can be changed to help cut down bullying is to group the classes together so that all classes of first year children are taught in the same area of the school. We think this minimises potential conflicts between the first year group (the most vulnerable year group in the school), and older children. We would like to arrange most of the school so that each year group has a suite of classrooms, but like most schools, we are limited by the architecture. Part of our aim, however, is to give the first year children a sense of ownership of their classroom areas, and we encourage them to look after their classrooms, to put displays on the wall, and to have their own set of games for wet lunchtimes.

The prefects were useful here as well. All the prefects were attached to a class, two of them to a first year class, and they would go over and spend lunchtimes in the first year classrooms. What tended to happen was that they looked after the younger children because they felt important, and they made sure that nobody else came into the classroom and bullied them. The development of positive relationships between the older children and the younger children gave both groups a structured understanding of their responsibilities to one another. Many of these developments arose pragmatically, rather than the whole system being thought out beforehand. We tried all sorts of ways of fostering this supportive situation between older children and younger children, such as helping them during their year assembly.

Using non-violent sanctions when incidents of bullying occur

If a school is to react effectively when particular incidents of bullying do occur, then the action taken needs to be in the same context of building a supportive ethos in school. The complete network of different features of school life described above are important in setting standards of what we expect of social life in school, and it is important that one particular situation does not cancel out what happens in another situation. The sanctions and general approaches used in dealing with children who bully must be based on principles similar to those used to set up a general school ethos as detailed above.

In practice, we have defined bullying very generally. It has included name calling, persistent minor harassment such as taking a pencil from someone and breaking it, as well as the more traumatic major incidents involving physical violence. The children perceive somebody who has knocked their bag over and kicked it round the classroom on more than one occasion as bullying. This leads to school staff spending a lot of time taking notice of a lot of apparently small things, and taking it seriously when a child says 'He has been calling me names'. If action is not taken at this level, the school is never going to do anything about actually changing the attitudes of children or really changing the amount of bullying that is occuring inside school. If the children get support on the minor incidents from staff, then they begin to believe that the support is also available for the more major ones.

For the staff to be seen to take bullying seriously, even with apparently small incidents, time has to be available, and there has to be a senior member of staff involved, a deputy head, the head or a head of schools. If the senior members of staff are seen as giving up their time to be involved it is therefore serious in the children's eyes. The full identification of those children involved, the discussions to unravel what actually happened, and working out of appropriate sanctions with the children concerned, can easily take an hour or even two. By the time the staff have talked to the victim, and found out who else was there, who saw or heard it happening, who else joined in; and have talked to the bully and he has said 'Well, it wasn't just me it was so and so as well', you might easily end up talking with ten to fifteen students. Then the staff involved – often two staff – have to get all the children together, and describe the best-fit version of the facts of the situation. From this point on we use group work techniques to explore how the victims felt, the bystanders' involvement or lack of it, the bully's motivations, and the feelings of the bully's friends who had been involved on his side as it were; and we work through the situation to the point where the bully is asked to say, if they were the headteacher, what would they suggest that the bully did to put things right?

In this sense the 'corrective' action seems some kind of atonement. It could be seen as a punishment but it isn't a punishment in the normal sense of the word. If for example there has been damage done to property, the bully will often suggest that they bring some money to buy another pencil case, or whatever. It isn't seen by the children that the school is imposing a punishment because they are naughty; rather they as individuals needed to do something to re-establish harmonious relationships.

It is not left at that. We then make a contract between the children whereby after they leave the room the victim obviously understands that if anything else happens then they can talk about it. Also the bully has a contract that he mustn't indulge in this kind of behaviour again, and the rest of the people in the room are actually given the responsibility of monitoring the situation. We say to them, 'Look, you know what has happened between these two. You are their friends, you're in their class, now you are going to be able to know if things are not going right and you are going to come and tell me and monitor the situation before it gets bad again'. And the children do do that. They are sent away with a task and responsibility and because they understand that, they go away feeling that they are quite important and have a job to do. They may come to us a few weeks later and say 'I think that maybe Johnny is upsetting Steven again'.

When talking with children about such an incident, our idea is to get them to think about a situation which might have happened to them and to respond to how *they* might feel. We are talking about a situation that has arisen and how to put it right. We are not talking in the end about who is going to leave the room and be given a punishment, and who is going to leave the room and feel that justice has been done. We are talking about, in the end, how to get to be friends again, or if not friends, relaxed acquaintances. The purpose of the session is to alter children's attitudes so that the same incident does not happen again, but also to ensure that it if did staff would get to know about it. In that way the session becomes a re-affirmation of those same standards of social behaviour that we have tried to make clear we expect in other aspects of school life, as well as a means of working towards acceptance of some sanctions, or other means of atonement for the hurtful actions.

In addition to this group session with the children directly or indirectly involved, we have also established an understanding with all pupils that the staff will see their parents, in all circumstances. Staff would always see the parents of a child who had been a bully and the parents of the child who had been their victim. We see each set of parents with their own child, and discuss the positive things that might happen at home that might help their sons or daughters not get into these situations again. We had always made it clear to both parents and children that should any incidents of bullying occur, both sets of parents would inevitably be informed and involved in the subsequent actions, so it is crucial that these promises are always kept.

Following these meetings at the time of the bullying incident, we may also arrange for longer term follow-up, either longer term group work for the victim, for the bully, or even individual counselling sessions involving internal members of staff or members of outside agencies. These have been discussed elsewhere (Foster, Arora and Thompson, 1990).

The amount of time spent in these discussions with children at first seemed daunting. However, one of the most irritating forms of children's behaviour in school is precisely those repeated but possibly minor incidents of disruptive behaviour aimed at other class members, and most staff approve of the time spent in properly tackling these things which are very important in terms of the atmosphere of the school. The frequently repeated minor incidents can cause much more accumulated stress to children and staff alike than do the occasional major one.

Support for teaching staff

Dealing with bullying in the way described here makes certain demands on teaching staff. To deal effectively with these situations, teachers need to have some skill with group work techniques, where issues are explored in ways which involve the emotional reaction of children as well as the specific agenda which needs to be communicated. A second area of skill is what are best described as counselling skills, the ability to work through highly emotionally charged situations with one or two individuals, or a child and his parents. Counselling skills give a certain confidence in working with highly emotional situations, and an understanding of how constructive end points can be reached. Dealing with children and their parents in situations which involve counselling skills of this nature is a specialised function for a few members of staff whose interests, training or school role have enabled them to learn how to deal with such situations. The group work skills on the other hand, are much more widely spread amongst people in most schools, and are teaching skills which are often used in ordinary lessons. The pastoral curriculum in particular encourages teachers to use group work methods.

To support staff in learning and using both these sets of skills, training opportunities have to be provided through workshops in school on inservice training days, through sending staff to external courses, and through being aware of the need for teachers to practice their new skills in situations where they are supported by the presence of more senior members of staff. The PSHE lessons are particularly important in developing the group work skills, and on occasions in the past when we have had adequate staffing we have arranged for some double staffing for PSHE lessons. One of the important things in successful implementation of an anti-bullying policy is that no member of staff should be put in sensitive situations with children or parents if they have not had some experience of learning how to deal with such situations. Finding supportive experiences is not too difficult, as it basically involves remembering to include an inexperienced member of staff in any group work which occurs, on an ad hoc basis, along with more experienced staff. As well as the need for specific support when dealing with children and parents, staff also need general support from the senior management team to help them maintain these interpersonal standards. Senior staff need to demonstrate through their behaviour the standards and integrity of communication leading to supportive social relationships that they wish to become the accepted standards of behaviour throughout the school.

CHAPTER 3

Developing a School Court as a Means of Addressing Bullying in Schools

Joan Brier and Yvette Ahmad

Our interest in bullying evolved from a long standing interest in the behaviour and social development of children in the primary years in general, particularly the children living in inner city areas of deprivation. One of us (J.B.) had previously developed a programme of Problem Solving Approaches to Social Development for an M.Ed. dissertation (Brier, 1988), and this formed the basis for a whole school approach to dealing with behaviour, and pro-active work through the whole curriculum, in the school of which I am Headteacher. However the constant problem of bullying outside the classroom, in the playground and outside school hours and school regime, was an ever present feature of most days. It seemed that we were unable to make significant inroads to improve the situation as regards bullying, despite having done so in the general behaviour of most of the children in the school for most of the time.

The bullying problem fell into four main categories:

(1) Children bringing into school incidents of bullying which had arisen in an out-of-school situation.
(2) Incidents of bullying which had taken place in the playground before school and at break times (particularly lunch times when there was minimum teacher presence).
(3) Incidents arising in the classroom from in-school situations.
(4) Children bullying teachers through classroom behaviours. Incidents of (3) and (4) seemed much less frequent than (1) and (2), especially with established staff, and mainly arose with supply/relief staff.

I found that most of the children knew what was right and accepted what was not, and could apply this knowledge within the school situation and ethos on most occasions, but were unable or unwilling to generalise this to other situations, mainly the home culture.

There were particular 'pockets' of bullying behaviour in certain year groups who appeared to have distinct attitude differences to those in more socially adjusted groups. This needed some investigation to address the problem effectively. In discussions with the LEA Adviser for Special Needs about the response of the LEA to the Elton Report on Discipline in Schools, I was offered some release time in order to make a more relevant study which could be of practical use to local schools.

A number of studies had addressed bullying behaviour in children, and this was where I started. The literature on the whole confirmed my ideas on the beginnings of bullying and some made suggestions as to how to deal with the problem. However, the main bulk of the literature was concerned with the post-primary child and remediation, whereas I was involved with children in the primary sector and was concerned with attitude development and pro-active measures. I have always been concerned about an over-emphasis on remediation for adverse behaviours, whereas research on child development indicates that early intervention in a pro-active manner is more effective, of long term effect, and is considerably less costly in both financial and personnel terms.

In my search of the literature I found confirmation and clarification of my understanding of the nature and origins of bullying in children. From this I constructed a model of our particular problem, the causes, and the possible ways in which we could develop an integrated programme of working with our children and possibly their families.

I had been having working discussions with a team of teachers who were working with a mixed group of Year 5 and Year 6 pupils grouped in three classes. These children as a whole had always presented some problems from Nursery age, but the main problem seemed to stem from a disproportionate group of boys who adopted a very physical, aggressive masculine 'style' and a group of verbally volatile females. They created a continuous undercurrent in which a relatively small occurrence could erupt into a major incident, while the rest of the group, though getting involved from time to time, were on the whole separate from these groups.

The characteristics of a bullying culture in the local environment (Dunning *et al.*, 1988) were very familiar and served to emphasise the enormity of our task. We identified in the local culture each of these characteristics:

- the local community is made up of an aggregate of structurally similar groups.
- maintaining ties with an unusually wide range of kin who live in the immediate locality.
- the community is strongly cohesive with narrow social horizons and a hostile attitude to outsiders.
- most salient emotional links are with others like themselves.
- adults in the community have positive attitudes to aggression (children are encouraged to 'stand up for themselves').
- parenting practices are highly influential in controlling/encouraging aggressive behaviour.
- low levels of supervision/monitoring.
- socialisation of the child mainly takes place on neighbourhood streets, where the child only has equally young or slightly older role models.
- physical prowess is valued more than academic achievement.

The chronic problem of bullying was becoming acute with this group of children and while acknowledging the need to work in an on-going manner on the social development and understandings of these children we had to address the problem in a more direct manner. To put the school's situation and my own impressions of the dimensions and causes of the problem into some sort of perspective, I talked to other professionals about their ideas and experiences on both the cause and effects of bullying. I undertook a series of discussions and interviews with a wide range of colleagues, including Social Workers, Educational Psychologists, Police Officers from the Child Abuse and Sexual Offences Unit, Child Abuse Counsellors, Education Social Workers from the LEA, colleagues in similar circumstances and members of the Department of Psychology at Sheffield University who were working on the measurement of the incidence of bullying in schools. From these discussions I agreed to pilot the questionnaire developed by Yvette Ahmad and Peter Smith (see Chapter 10), in order to document further the size and focus of the problem in the school. All children in Year 4 to Year 7 (7 classes in all) were involved in the survey, which was first given in January by Yvette Ahmad, and the results confirmed our impressions of the extent and location of the problem.

Summary of questionnaire results

○ About 29 per cent of the children reported being bullied 'sometimes' or 'several times a week'. This was a high percentage – about half as much again as the average so far for primary schools in the South Yorkshire Area (Ahmad and Smith, 1990).

○ About 14 per cent of children report bullying others – again high, about twice the usual percentage.

○ Sex differences followed the usual pattern. Boys bullied more than girls, both sexes were victims equally.

○ There were marked class variations. All three classes in Year 5/6, and one class in Year 4, reported high levels of being bullied. Both Year 7 classes and the other Year 4 class, reported much lower levels.

○ Most bullying occurred in the playground, usually by other children in the same year group.

○ Much of it was name-calling. Some was hitting, and there was a wide variety of other forms reported.

○ More pupils than usual had told teachers or parents about being bullied, but still quite a large number had not done so.

○ Many children said they would wish to help a child being bullied, even if they were not often seen as doing so. A majority were upset by bullying or found it difficult to understand. Thus, even though the problem was worse in this school than in many others, it might still be possible to mobilise peer group opinion further against bullying.

The decision to focus on the three vertically grouped Year 5/Year 6 classes to address the bullying problem had already been taken and this decision was confirmed by the questionnaire results. The input was to be a part of a topic project on 'Our Bodies and Ourselves'. The work was to be with small groups of about eight children and I aimed to address the issues of bullying behaviour and of victim behaviour in these groups separately. To this end we assigned each of the children in the target group (71 children) into one of six categories (see Figure 3.1).

The three teachers involved discussed each child individually and then came to an agreement about the category appropriate to that child's normal behaviour. The results were worrying and underlined our concerns. These children were then placed into eight groups: 5 contained a mix of children in the bully categories with some in the normal category and 3 groups constituted a mix of victims and normal category children. I worked with each group in 30 to 45 minute sessions on about three or four occasions on social development and co-operative games appropriate to the needs of each group. This enabled a lot of discussion, some opening up of thought processes, and the examination and forming of attitudes and opinions.

The effects were not formally measured in any way, but there was no noticeable behaviour change as far as we could see. However, I feel in retrospect that any following success was built on the shared understanding arrived at in these sessions and that it was a necessary process in getting the children to have some objectivity in the work which followed. All through this time we continue to address the problems arising in the day to day life of school through the Problem Solving formula, developed as the mainstay of the schools' social development programme (Brier, 1988), together with the insistence

A. Average:
   – neither bullies nor victims.

B. Bullies:
   – physically strongest of all categories,
   – active,
   – assertive,
   – easily provoked,
   – enjoy situations with aggressive content,
   – a positive attitude to violence underlies behaviour.

C. Anxious Bullies:
   – mainly male,
   – lack of confidence,
   – have few likable qualities,
   – frequently have problems at home,
   – poor attainment and/or concentration,
   – insecure and unpopular,
   – have educational difficulties,
   – bully in an attempt to compensate for feelings of inadequacy.

D. Victims:
   – passive individuals,
   – lacking in self-confidence,
   – unpopular,
   – physically weaker/smaller than most children,
   – frequently do not complain.

E. Provocative Victims:
   – more assertive/active/confident than other victims,
   – actively provoke bullying,
   – (often create considerable management problems).

F. Bully/Victims:
   – children who both bully and are themselves bullied,
   – least popular with other children,
   – physically stronger than their victims,
   – more assertive than their victims,
   – easily provoked,
   – frequently provoke others.

Figure 3.1 Categories of bullies and victims (from Stephenson and Smith, 1989)

that the most important factor in the whole equation of unacceptable behaviour was for the victim to tell the relevant authority figure so that appropriate action could be taken.

My attention was then drawn to the use of Bully Courts in schools (Laslett, 1982; Pavey, 1990) by our local Community Police Inspector, and the possibility of adopting this strategy was discussed with the teachers concerned with the high bullying classes. Our approach was to put the proposal to the children and to then develop the idea with a small group of representatives. The representatives were elected by the children, three from each of the Year 5/6 classes, nine representatives in all. There was discussion about the appropriate criteria for selection; the basic criteria arrived at were that the representatives should be honest, fair and not easily influenced by others. There was also concern that the representatives could be open to bullying themselves and that bullies may try to use their influence in getting the group to use their power over other children. It was interesting and reassuring to find that the children elected all fell into the 'normal' or 'victim' categories in the earlier assessment.

The form of preparation was to discuss initially the basic construction of the judicial system and try to ally this with the constraints of our own school situation. I was able to arrange for the children to visit the local Crown Court to see the layout of a court room and to talk to one of the Court Police Officers. (This was not easy to arrange as there are strict rules governing children under 14 entering the courts, and it appeared to be more difficult to visit a Magistrates Court than the Crown Court. It is not possible for children under 14 to go into a session.) However, from this visit the children had a much clearer image of the sort of situation and organisation we would need to develop.

Simple statement and summons forms were designed (see Figure 3.2) and procedures were agreed by the planning group of the nine representatives elected by their peers, and then presented to the whole group for their approval. The procedure for any complaint was that in the initial stage the first approach should be to the complainant's teacher. This was in order to avoid trivial disputes being brought to the School Court, and to reserve court appearances for more serious offences. The teachers would then use their judgement as to whether the incident was to be dealt with within the classroom situation or whether it was more serious and warranted taking to the School Court. The pupil making the complaint and those who were being charged were then obliged to give statements of the events in question on the

SCHOOL COURT

===

DATE: 25th September, 1990

Name: ....

Date of Offence:..

Offence: ....

....

You are summoned to appear before this court on:

Date: .... Time: ....

Place: ....

Signed: ....

       Clerk to the Court.

===

===

SCHOOL COURT

===

STATEMENT

DATE: 25th September, 1990

Name: ....

Date of alleged offence:...

Statement:...

....

....

....

....

....

....

....

....

Signed: .... date: ....

Figure 3.2 Summons form and statement form for a bully court

statement forms, which were then submitted to me as the Court Officer. The time and date of the hearing was arranged by me and the parents of the children concerned were informed of the proposed hearing.

The preparation for the pupils who had been elected to the Bench was, we realised later, insufficient in the initial stages and needed extending. The members of the Bench were probably more overwhelmed than those summoned to appear before them, and it was necessary to do role-plays and prepare questions in advance to ensure a well conducted hearing. In the event, these first courts were more teacher-led than we would have wished. However, the closing discussion was detailed and we were impressed by the fairness and objectivity the children demonstrated in their discussions, particularly in view of the fact that all those involved were well known to them.

In the first five weeks of the court only two cases were heard. The Bench consisted of two teachers and five of the nine elected pupils. The layout of the room was as close to the court layout as possible, but we did not allow any audience into the hearing, in line with practice in Juvenile Court. The complainant was first to give evidence and the members of the Bench were able to ask questions about their statement. Then the Defendant(s) were called separately and the Complainant as well as the Bench were allowed to ask questions of them about the incident. After this the Bench discussed the matter in private and came to their conclusions. The vexed problem of punishments then came into consideration. We had previously talked about the sanctions and punishments which were appropriate to the sort of problems we were considering, and the problems of supervision and monitoring. At first the children had been fairly Draconian in their proposed punishments but had then, with help, moderated their ideas to more workable and appropriate levels. The sort of sanctions used were, clearing the playground of rubbish for a week, or losing a chance to go to out-of-school activities. Although the punishments were fairly low-level, and considered necessary, it appeared to us that it was the court appearance which was the main deterrent for most children. The pupils passing sentence were also supervisors to see that the punishments were carried out in a satisfactory manner.

At the end of the term we spent some time with each of the three classes doing a de-brief session, where I asked for impressions of the workability and effect of the Court, how it could be improved, whether we should continue in the same way, if improvements could be made, whether we should extend to consider a wider range of misdemeanours than bullying.

The children were sure that the presence of the Court in school had had a positive effect, and some claimed they had been able to use the threat of taking bullies to the Court to curb bullying activities. There was a five week period to the end of term when there were no cases brought to the Court, and some of the children from time to time mentioned that it was being effective (although we as teachers were not quite so sure). However, it was felt strongly by a large number of children that there had been a clear increase in the incidence of bullying in the outside school situation. Some discussion centred around the possibility of the Court hearing complaints which had occurred outside school hours and premises, but for many reasons I felt I had to veto this idea.

The survey service was carried out again by Yvette Ahmad, on the whole of the Middle School age children, in July, about seven months after the first survey. Since the interventions (group work and School Court) had been with the three classes in Years 5/6, but not with the two classes in Year 4 or the two classes in Year 7, it was possible to compare changes in those classes which had, or had not, received the intervention.

The results of this are shown in Figure 3.3, separately for reports of being bullied, and of bullying others. For simplicity, and following usual practice, we have summed the responses 'sometimes' and 'several times a week' as indicating that bullying has occurred, and the responses 'only once or twice' or 'I haven't bullied/been bullied' as

	Average for 3 intervention classes: years 5/6	Average for 4 non-intervention classes: years 4, and 7
	(a) percent reporting being bullied	
Before intervention	42.2	16.8
After intervention	35.0	19.7
	(b) percent reporting bullying others	
Before intervention	17.2	10.8
After intervention	12.3	12.2

Figure 3.3 Levels of bullying reported in intervention and non-intervention classes, at two time points

indicating that it has not occurred (at least to a serious extent). There is considerable class variation, so the results are summed over the four Year 4 and Year 7 classes which did not get the intervention, and the three Year 5/6 classes which did.

As can be seen from Figure 3.3, there is some indication that the intervention had an effect. Levels of bullying in the Years 5/6 were clearly very high to start with (hence we had chosen to work with them); but had fallen by 7 per cent. Similarly, levels of reported bullying others had fallen by 5 per cent. Given the limited scale of the intervention, this is encouraging.

It might be that these changes were due to factors other than the intervention; for example children getting older, or a different time of school year for testing. However, the results for the non-intervention classes provide a kind of 'control' for this. In these classes in fact there was a slight increase in reported problems, by about 3 per cent in the case of being bullied, and 1–2 per cent in the case of bullying others. This does suggest that the relative change in the Year 5/6 classes was not due to factors such as age or time of year, or even changes in the understanding of the questionnaire, which would probably have affected all classes similarly.

What can be learned from this is that an intervention such as using a School Court, can have an impact but does need to be employed throughout the whole school for the impact to be significant. Taking a positive approach to bullying is not an easy line to follow if school and teachers are expected to solve all anti-social problems. For any positive action to be significantly effective it has to include teachers, parents, school governors, dinner supervisors and other society members where possible.

It must be stressed that this school takes an active and positive approach to bullying. The school has a whole school policy of positive action against bullying and all anti-social behaviour. The teachers stress to all their pupils that this is a telling school and this was reflected in the initial survey results in that more pupils told their teachers about being bullied in comparison to many other schools.

At the beginning of the next school year the staff had discussions as to whether to continue the School Court; to extend the Court to all the children in the school; to extend the Court's remit to a wider range of unacceptable behaviours. Our conclusion was that we should continue the Court; we should extend the range of behaviours to be dealt with; that we try to build on the work put in earlier. However, we could not afford the amount of time which had been necessary in the early stages particularly in view of the demands being made on both teachers and pupils through the National Curriculum. Indeed, without the additional time allowed in the beginning of the project it would never have got off the ground. In view of this workload we decided that we would have to exclude teachers from the running of the Court hearings and only hold the Court in out-of-lesson time. I would be the only adult involved and would carry out the necessary training and organisation. New representatives were elected from each class and I had to do specific preparation for these new members.

My own conclusion is, that the most important benefit comes from the *process* of organising and developing the Court. Through the discussions and examination involved, the children were enabled to look at themselves and their group and started to have some understanding of the behaviours and differences of attitude between individuals. They were able to gain some understanding of the process of law and the need for codes of conduct and sanctions and they began to realise the difficulties of coming to fair and evenhanded conclusions, and were able to develop some skills in listening to varied accounts of a single event and coming to some sort of agreed consensus opinion. I also feel that the background of social development which is very strong in the school and runs through the whole curriculum and organisation of the establishment, is a necessary precursor for any degree of success. The children have a good background experience of talking through situations and being made to consider their actions within a whole event.

Further consideration will have to be given, from time to time, to maintaining the interest in and credibility of the Court; to prepare new representatives elected to the Bench; and to monitoring the effectiveness of the Court on the conduct of the children. I have some concerns that the Court is, to some degree, a negative sanction and may be contrary to the positive developmental ethos which we try to adopt at all times in the school. However, a respect for basic rules and consideration for others and their property is fundamental to both the school and the social structure in which the school and the community exist. Adherence to basic rules is necessary for a well ordered society, and within our own culture those not respecting these rules are dealt with through the court system. As a fact of life, children should have some knowledge and understanding from an early age of the potential consequence of anti-social action.

It was very hard work, but in the final analysis probably worth the effort, as long as a balance is struck between the social and the

CHAPTER 4

The Use of Victim Support Groups

Tiny Arora

This chapter forms a detailed description of the issues involved in setting up a support group for victims of bullying. It aims to provide a practical framework which will help in the initial discussions, the planning of the group's aims and objectives, the contents of the sessions and the evaluation. It is written with secondary school pupils in mind, especially those in Years 7 to 9, as the author has been mostly involved in groupwork with this age range. Most issues discussed below, however, apply equally to children who are both younger and older.

Aim of such groups

A whole range of interventions aimed at reducing bullying are available to schools, from a whole school approach (Foster *et al.*, 1990) to 'on the spot' actions by an individual teacher (Arora, 1989). Regular support for victims will provide yet another means of tackling the problem. The aim of such a support group would be to change the status of the children from being victims to belonging to the non-bullied and non-bullying group, which constitutes the majority of pupils in the school (normally at least 75 per cent). This can be achieved through teaching the skills required to deal effectively with bullying and how to avoid being bullied. At the same time the group can provide encouragement and opportunities for mutual support and possibly friendships.

Make-up of the groups

With limited resources available, it is preferable to concentrate on helping the victims rather than trying to stop the bullies' actions. There are a variety of reasons for this; in the first place it is usually much easier to teach new behaviours rather than stop or replace already established behaviours. Thus, victims could be taught new strategies to cope with or avoid bullying. Bullies, on the other hand, need to be persuaded to stop or change their actions, which is much more difficult to achieve. Secondly, the bully's behaviour is at the least tacitly condoned in many situations and often also actively encouraged or modeled. Olweus (1978) has pointed to the home background as an influential factor associated with bullying: bullies often had parents who themselves had been bullies and were frequently brought up in an atmosphere of aggression. It is therefore likely that the parents have acted as models for their own children to copy. Similarly, teachers have suggested that teacher–pupil bullying (and vice-versa) does occur in most school systems, thereby providing powerful role models for pupils. In view of the above it is not surprising that most bullies are generally confident and quite convinced that violence and coercion are legitimate means of establishing social dominance in their group (Bjorkqvist *et al.*, 1982). Bullies have also learnt (unless effective intervention and prevention have been carried out) that their actions usually bring reward, which, as basic psychology theory suggests, makes their behaviour very resistant to change.

It would therefore be reasonable to conclude that changing bullies' behaviour could be difficult to achieve. A far more promising avenue would be to try to deprive the bullies of easy rewards by working intensively with the victims.

It is not suggested here that one should never work therapeutically with bullies. On the contrary, it is essential that interventions are carried out with this group as well and some of these are covered in this book. However, given possible limitations of time and other resources, concentrating on the victims is likely to effect the most positive change.

Should one mix victims and bullies?

There are strong reasons for advocating that the group should consist of victims only. Before outlining these reasons it must be pointed out that not everyone agrees with this view. Some people argue that mixing a group of victims and bullies provides an opportunity for learning directly about each other's feelings and motives and would therefore create greater awareness and sensitivity and make bullying less likely. Verbal reports have been received claiming that such groups can be run successfully. It is up to the reader to decide what seems to be most appropriate. It is certainly recommended to have victim/bully/bystander sessions in the wake of an actual incident (Foster *et al.*, 1990) but for groups with a more long-term goal this does not seem desirable.

By having only victims in the group it should be possible to cater more specifically for their needs. The majority of victims are described as passive, lacking in confidence and often physically weaker than other children. A small subgroup of victims are 'provocative': they don't share the above characteristics and tend to be more active and easily provoked themselves (Stephenson and Smith, 1989). To mix these children in a group with bullies, who are more confident and enjoy aggression, puts them at a distinct disadvantage. A further reason for excluding bullies is that a teaching programme to help victims, which might include assertiveness training and self protection, does not necessarily focus on the needs of bullies.

Should boys and girls be in the same group?

There would seem to be differences in the ways boys and girls are bullied. Boys appear to tease and use physical violence the most, whilst girls may also tease but most often practise exclusion from the peer group (Roland, 1989). Girls seem to engage more often in 'psychological' bullying whilst boys tend to use direct physical methods. This points to the need to separate the two sexes if one wishes to teach the victims methods of coping with the specific types of bullying to which they are subject. An argument against this is that mixed gender teaching is now so common in most of our school systems that pupils themselves may feel slightly uncomfortable if they are separated into single sex groupings for no apparent reason.

How many in a group?

The size of the group depends on the number of adults available and on the group members to be selected. Ideally a ratio of one adult to three or four children is recommended, particularly when a number of provocative victims are involved. A good working group is six to eight children with two adults. This provides flexibility for small groupwork, working in pairs and short periods of whole groupwork, to be extended to longer periods as the group becomes more cohesive.

How are the group members selected?

A mixture of methods is the most reliable for ensuring that all victims are considered for possible selection from the particular school population which is the focus of the intervention. A questionnaire completed by the pupils themselves, which asks specific questions about whether they have been bullied (Ahmad and Smith, 1990) or whether they were at the receiving end of a large number of aggressive actions or threats from their peers (Arora and Thompson, 1987) could be the main source of information. If this is further combined with asking both teachers and pupils to identify victims in a confidential survey, the broadest results will be yielded. The reasons for this are that not all victims will report that they are bullied and teachers tend to underestimate the number of victims in their care as they do not often witness any bullying incidents.

Voluntary rather than compulsory attendance at the sessions is recommended. This will ensure that only motivated pupils attend and will provide the group leaders with an immediate feedback of how helpful the work has been to those initially selected.

Who should be the group leaders?

Ideally, group leaders should be people with a knowledge of the complexities of bullying, experience of groupwork and an interest in social skills training. The work is best done by those who have daily contact with the pupils, i.e. the teaching staff of the particular school, but they could be augmented by members of the support services who are experienced or have an interest in this work, such as educational psychologists, support teachers, and social workers.

Who needs to be prepared?

It is important that the victims themselves are given clear reasons for their selection as possible group members, without further decreasing their already low self-esteem (Bjorkqvist et al., 1982). It will not be necessary to identify their status as victims as the sole reason. Most of them will already be aware that they are in need of some support, particularly from fellow pupils. This may be given as the main reason for forming the group. If its contents and objectives are also outlined, the pupils will be able to make a more informed choice than if they are simply told that it is a group for victims of bullying. It may also be possible at this stage to engage the pupil in a discussion as to what s/he would like to learn in the group.

The parents of the pupils need to be informed and their consent obtained if the group is not part of the normal school curriculum. Even if the group is part of the curriculum it will benefit from having the active backing of the parents. Research has indicated that the parents of bullied children tend to be overprotective and rather anxious themselves (Olweus, 1978) so it is of some help to them to know that specific action is being taken to support their children and help them to relate with others.

All the staff who are having contact with the pupils concerned need to be informed prior to the start of the session. It is often helpful to gather their comments on the pupils, especially in relation to the particular strengths and weaknesses they may have in social situations, so that these can be used as part of a base for programming the course. The use of a checklist (Spence, 1977) could assist this procedure. Many staff will also find it helpful to know what the contents will be on a weekly basis so that particular teaching points can be incorporated into cross-curricular activities.

Group meetings and activities

How often, when and where?

Realistically, weekly sessions are the most frequent that can be managed during school term time. Sessions could be run entirely during the school day but this may put restrictions on an already tight curriculum. They could also be run out of school hours but this may be seen by some pupils as too demanding due to other competing demands such as homework, jobs (for secondary school pupils) or club activities. One compromise could be to run a session which takes some time off the end of the school day and to combine this with time immediately after school finishes. This will then give the message to the pupils that some contribution is expected from themselves as well as from the school.

The duration of the session will depend on a number of factors, such as the age and attention span of the group members, the time that can be made available and the number of staff involved. It can be tempting to designate a regular form period for this purpose, but in many schools this is too short a time to utilise effectively for this purpose. The minimum time to set aside for groupwork of this type is 45 minutes, with a maximum of 90 minutes. One-hour sessions will usually cover most of the contents that one would wish to include.

The number of sessions required depends partly on their length. It will be necessary to develop a gradual programme which aims to teach a number of skills and to create a cohesive support group for all the pupils (see below) which takes time. A group needs time to 'gel' and to become a genuinely supportive and effective vehicle for change. A total of 12 hours of time spent together would be considered the minimum, with any further extension of this extremely productive. The resources of the school will ultimately determine the number of sessions in any course.

It is important to establish a regular and comfortable venue for the group. Although this can be difficult in a school in which space is at a premium, it will greatly contribute to a successful outcome for the group.

Contents of the sessions

The aim of a victim support group would be to teach the pupils those skills which are common to non-bullied children and which would help them to become members of the latter category. This would include strategies to deal with bullying when it occurs and to avoid situations in which bullying is likely to happen.

For the purpose of deciding on the group's objectives and, therefore, on its contents, it is necessary to consider how bullied and non-bullied children differ from each other. It has already been noted that frequent victims of bullying are commonly weaker and smaller than other pupils. They are also often less attractive physically (Lowenstein, 1978). There is not a great deal one can do about such physical characteristics. There are, however, other features which are related to social and interpersonal skills and which are significant for the programme of a support group. Non-bullied children are, relative to bullied children:

○ More sensitive to feelings of others and more ready to help to protect others.
○ Less selfish and kinder.

○ Better adjusted and more capable of controlling their feelings.
○ More effective in joining in with others in work and more conforming to the norms.
○ Less excessively dominating, aggressive, boastful or attention seeking.
○ Less excessively demanding of others to do things for them.
○ More often taught by their parents to consider others and not merely themselves.
○ More willing to retaliate.

(Lowenstein, 1978)

It has already been mentioned that victims of bullying have low self-esteem. The majority of victims tend to be passive but a small proportion of these tend to be provocative (Stephenson and Smith, 1989) and to retaliate easily but often ineffectively.

These features provide pointers to a wealth of materials to include in a programme for the group, particularly in the area of social skills. Those familiar with the contents of social skills training will recognise that these usually cover a number of areas which are pertinent to the needs of victims, such as:

○ Awareness of own feelings/emotions and those of others.

(Remocker and Storch, 1987)

○ How to be positive about oneself without boasting.

(McConnon, 1989a)

○ How to work co-operatively with others.

(Masheder, 1986)

○ How to maintain friendships.

(McConnon, 1989b and c)

○ How to deal with conflict.

(Judson, 1984)

○ How to stand up for yourself.

(Elliott, 1986; Hopson and Scally, 1980)

○ How to use 'non-victim' body language.

(Neill, 1991)

Other areas which can be covered in the group are:

- relaxation training (Saunders and Remsberg, 1986)
- teaching assertiveness skills (Hopson and Scally, 1980; Northumberland Ed. Dept., 1989)
- rational emotive therapy (Dryden, 1989).

The latter is a means of reinterpreting in a more rational way what is happening to you. Children who overreact to teasing and taunting will be unable to change their behaviour unless they can reason that the whole world is not coming to an end if someone calls them names or that it is not necessary to be loved by everyone.

In choosing the contents of the sessions it is important not to lose sight of the more immediate aim for the group, i.e. to help them cope with bullying or avoid situations in which this may happen. One way in which to avoid being bullied is to stay close to friends who are ready to protect the potential victim if necessary. It is therefore particularly important to work on friendship skills, both on how to make friends and on how to maintain friendships.

In connection with the same aims it will be necessary to make the victims aware that there are a variety of responses possible to bullying and also to give them the experience to practise those so that they have

---

1. Name Calling
You have just come out of French and are on your way to P.E. Whilst walking through the corridor you see ahead of you two boys who are messing about and calling names to many pupils who pass.

● Think of as many things as possible which you could do or say.

● Choose the best three to act out.

---

2. Demanding Money
(a) You are in the playground, standing by yourself, when two bigger boys come up to you and start to push you, saying they want 50p off you. They know that you have the money on you.

(b) How can you deal with this situation now? Write down as many ways as possible, choose the best two to act out and explain why these are the best ones.

---

3. A holding threat
Some of your classmates are threatening to hold you back after school/during breaks for no apparent reason. They have done this once before and it made you very upset.

● What can you do? Write down as many answers as you can think of.

● Choose the best two to act out.

---

4. Hitlist
One boy/girl accuses you of splitting on him/her to the Year head. You have now been put on the 'hitlist' of his/her friends.

● How do you deal with this? Who can help? Who else do you need to talk to?

● Show two different ways in which you might solve this problem.

Figure 4.1 Examples of bullying situations for small group work

a range of strategies at their disposal. A valuable means of introduction is a 'real bullying situation' which is given on a card to a small group with the request to consider alternative responses and act some of these out in front of the entire group. Figure 4.1 provides a number of examples.

Productive limitation of aims and contents

It is tempting to pack the course with a wide content variety. This could lead to a very checkered programme which does not really address the specific needs of the children involved. It is better to choose only two or three objectives for the entire course and to fit in the contents accordingly. Setting clear objectives is also essential for an effective evaluation (see below). Once the pupils to take part in the course have been selected it will become clearer what the objectives for the group should be, especially if account is taken of the pupils' preferences expressed in the initial individual discussion. Further details on the pupils' social skills may be collected through checklists completed by the staff (Spence, 1977) and by pen pictures provided by their form teachers.

One support group had the following aims and objectives:

> To select a group of pupils who are often at the receiving end of aggressive actions and/or threats from other pupils and to use groupwork methods to teach them (a) to become more aware of different ways of relating to other pupils, (b) to see themselves more positively and (c) to feel more in control of their own actions and reactions. The overall aim is to reduce the number of times that the pupils are bullied.

Which methods of teaching are most suitable?

In deciding this one has to take account of the maturity of those participating, the number of adults involved and their relative status in the eyes of the pupils. As has been noted above, victims tend to lack the social skills required to co-operate in groups and it is therefore unlikely that whole-group work will be effective. A mixture of small group work and some individual work is likely to be most appropriate, with a very short whole-group activity which could be increased gradually as the group becomes more cohesive and more able to function co-operatively.

Role play has already been mentioned as one method. A variety of other methods should also be considered. The pupils should enjoy themselves but not become overexcited as might sometimes happen if they are not used to small group work. Games which teach various skills or make the participants aware of the different interpersonal skills required can be very useful. Individual or small group drawings are another means of making points or learning about each other.

Evaluation and follow-up

Running a small group with a high adult–pupil ratio is expensive, both in resources and time. It is therefore essential to evaluate whether these are well used. It is not sufficient for the group leader to feel a warm glow and a sense of achievement after the sessions have finished. Quantitative and qualitative data are necessary to decide whether the objectives for the group are being met. It is useful to obtain these data from a variety of sources and in a variety of ways. In that way, one piece of evidence might corroborate another and strengthen one's overall impression. If the data are conflicting then it would be wise to conclude that the outcome is not as successful as one might have hoped. The following methods of evaluation were used for the group whose aim and objectives were mentioned above:

(1) All the targeted pupils, along with the other pupils in their form, were asked to complete a checklist (Battle, 1981) in order to measure their self-esteem. The same pupils were asked to do so again after the group had finished. This provided a measure not only of the progress of the members of the group themselves, but also allowed a comparison with those who did not take part.

(2) At the beginning of each session, the pupils were asked to complete a checklist ('Life in School' – see Arora and Thompson, 1987) on which they had to tick what interactions they had had with other pupils during the previous week. These could be both negative and positive and included a direct question as to whether they had been bullied.

(3) At the end of each session and near the beginning of the next session, the adults involved evaluated what had happened and planned/prepared for the next session(s).

(4) After the group sessions had finished, staff were circulated with a checklist to indicate whether they had noted any changes in various aspects of the pupils' social behaviour.

(5) During the last session, each pupil was asked to complete an evaluation sheet under 'exam' conditions, to ascertain what they had learnt from the course, whether they had enjoyed it and whether they had any suggestions for improvements.

(6) The pupils' attendance to each session was recorded.

It would also have been informative to ask for the parents' opinions as to whether their child had benefited.

Follow-up

After the course and its evaluation has finished, the staff will need to be informed of the outcome, perhaps with a short report.

The pupils who participated could be given an acknowledgement that they have successfully completed the course. A well printed certificate will add status and increase self-esteem.

CHAPTER 5

Dealing with Bullying in a Special Needs Unit

Doris West

The Special Needs Section at Salisbury College of Technology provides Further Education for students between 16 and 19 years of age, and incorporates two full-time courses:

(1)   Vocational Preparation Studies for students with moderate learning difficulties.
(2)   Continuing Education for students with severe learning difficulties.

Young people with moderate learning difficulties have access to College courses and workshop facilities where they may integrate with mainstream students. They also have a distinctive study base located on the College campus which not only provides a supportive environment for those in need of extra help, but also gives students ownership of a particular College facility, and a focus for social activities and meetings.

Young people with severe learning difficulties who attend Salisbury College of Technology have access to similar facilities in addition to their own study base, and, where appropriate, integrate with other students to share projects and assignments. Both study bases are situated on the periphery of the campus and are equipped to facilitate a variety of practical and domestic activities.

Both courses offer a broad based experience within which students are encouraged to pursue individual learning programmes, each giving emphasis to the acquisition of confidence, knowledge and skills, at a level commensurate with each young person's ability and needs. Work experience, residential projects and a constructive approach to leisure enhance the curriculum and an active involvement in community projects is encouraged. Students also organise and run a mini-company (Minico) producing and marketing craft items in order to finance some of their projects.

A 'menu' of part time specialist courses designed to meet the needs of identified groups of people with moderate or severe learning difficulties and/or some kind of physical disability is an important part of the work of Salisbury College. These include:

○ School Links Courses which enable pupils from 'feeder' schools to attend College on one day a week to take part in integrated study projects.

○ Communication skills and Social competence: a modular course for people with moderate/severe learning difficulties.

○ Woodwork and related work skills: an assignment-based course for people who live in small group homes.

○ Computer Studies: for the recovering mentally ill.

○ Workshop skills for students with severe learning difficulties: a modular course incorporating construction, woodwork, pottery, gardening, and metal work.

Staff who are involved in teaching students with Special Education Needs have, where necessary, the support of a Care Assistant, and the work is co-ordinated by the Tutor/Organiser for Special Needs. A comprehensive Staff Development programme enables tutors working with students who have Special Education Needs to develop areas of study relevant to their work and disseminate information to their colleagues and other Colleges by way of seminars and workshops. As part of this process, in March 1989, I attended the first National Conference on Bullying presented in London by the Kidscape organisation and through this I became interested in the work of Michelle Elliot (Director of Kidscape) and others who are investigating this aspect of challenging behaviour.

The Conference did not give emphasis to young people with learning difficulties but my experience was to tell me that College students with Special Needs can be prime targets for bullying, not only amongst themselves, but also from other members of the public – at the bus station, and in the underpass, or when walking to and from College. At that busy time of day when many children are making their way home from school, students who have to cope with a disability or a handicap may be tired and less able to deal with harassment or teasing and are easily targeted by the opportunist bully.

During the day when moving about the campus from one location to another, along corridors, on the stairs, or in the toilets, the College environment offered students within the Special Needs groups plenty of opportunity to inflict upon each other behaviour intended to cause discomfort or distress. It was interesting to note that most mainstream students were found to be helpful and considerate towards students with Special Needs and that most cases of bullying behaviour occurred within the group or off the College campus.

Lists detailing aspects of behaviour or attitude likely to identify a potential victim of bullying will describe many students with Special Education Needs, for example: they may have a speech impediment or poor sight; in some cases they may be more noticeable by their behaviour or appearance, by race, size, or disability. Further Education provision for students with learning difficulties at the Salisbury College of Technology is, however, well supervised. It has a comprehensive programme of vocational and social skills training and personal development. It has an open, democratic ethos with emphasis on self-help, self respect and concern for others. With a curriculum based on interaction and responsibility, and aiming at enhancing the transition into young adulthood, how could bullying become a problem?

On the face of things there did not appear to be a problem – no one was complaining. There were, however, observed changes in behaviour that were causing concern, and a marked deterioration in the attitudes, responses and concentration of some students warranted investigation. Enquiries to parents offered no solution and we were unable to identify possible causes in the home. Members of the staff team who deal exclusively with students who have Special Education Needs meet with the Tutor/Organiser on a daily basis to discuss student concerns and the work of the day. It was in this way that we were able, collectively, to agree to observe the behaviour of these students and record the way in which they interacted with the rest of the group.

Within a week several instances of verbal harassment and 'it was only a joke' incidents had been highlighted. For example: when Neil twisted Alan's ear as he passed him in the cloakroom it was said to be a joke. This behaviour was not funny from Alan's point of view and he certainly wasn't laughing. It was agreed that if this, and other incidents, had not been observed by a member of staff they would not have been reported. Subsequently, a record of events, discussed at length by the staff team, indicated that:

○ Other students were being subjected to this kind of petty cruelty and the attacks were recurrent.

○ Verbal abuse, and deliberately orchestrated verbal harassment were taking place, e.g. students handicapped by obesity and speech impairment were particularly targeted by the bullies who lay in wait and followed them chanting abuse.

○ Two students within the group were supporting each other in behaviour that could be described as bullying.

○ One student, with considerable insight and manipulative ability was directing another to carry out physical attacks, and encouraging him to vandalise the property of other students.

○ This behaviour was being sustained by a conspiracy of silence.

The bullies were now known to us, and bullying incidents were being dealt with by the staff as and when we were able to spot them, but we needed to break into a code of silence which stipulated that telling tales is shameful. The measures at our disposal for dealing with this problem were clearly inadequate. We needed to open up the whole subject and extend it beyond the tripartite issue it had become between the staff, the victims, and the bullies, without putting students who were being discriminated against at risk.

In order to do this we decided that the subject of bullying would be introduced into a creative studies session, and with the use of a variety of art media, poems, newspaper articles and photographs it would be offered as a theme for expressive work.

A group of eighteen students, including the bullies, were encouraged to discuss the theme but most of them related incidents that had happened to someone else or 'a long time ago when I was at school'. When, on a later occasion, the students were divided into two smaller sub-groups and the bullies were separated between them, practical work got under way and became more personal. Areas of distress were highlighted.

Some students referred back to incidents that had occurred whilst they were still at school, some gave details of events that they had witnessed and told of their feelings of distress and helplessness, others illustrated what has been called 'mobbing' (Pikas, 1989) and several students illustrated current problems within the group. All the students were able to relate personally to the problems of bullying; some had been bullied at school but not at College whilst others were experiencing these problems for the first time.

The unsigned illustrations were later displayed and both groups, with members of staff, met together to discuss them. This is in no way unusual as we often meet to review the progress of shared projects. It is at these reflective sessions we find that learning is reinforced and students are encouraged to take an active part in negotiating the progression of their own work.

The bullying incidents on display formed a visual representation of a collective past and present experience shared by this group of students, and opened up the subject for discussion. Events and feelings were described and it was agreed that bullying was 'a bad thing' and that it is very difficult to deal with. It was also clear that these young people, most of whom wanted to be regarded as young adults, were reluctant to admit to having problems of this kind. As one student said:

> You come to College and try to act like an adult, but saying that you are being bullied is like being a school kid again. That's what happens at school. They (the bullies) are acting like school kids. They haven't changed.

For some students the hopes of a fresh start in a new environment away from the problems that had been encountered at school had not been fulfilled. Many of them had progressed through the educational system within reach of the same groups of children and had entered Further Education to find themselves having to work with people who had caused them distress in the past. Most students who had experienced bullying were aware of the difficulties in breaking out of an on-going cycle of victimisation or harassment that could be carried forward year by year.

Using art materials and the informality of a creative studies session had given us the opportunity to bring out into the open problems that had been thriving in secrecy. It had also given those students who were unable to communicate orally in an effective way the chance to have their say. In one way or another bullying has affected, or was affecting all the members of the group; witnessing such incidents has caused as much anxiety and distress to those who were not actively involved and a feeling of guilt was described by victims and bystanders alike which said:

- if I am being bullied it must be my fault
- if I am being bullied I will just have to put up with it
- if I say that bullying is taking place I'll look like a tell-tale
- if I say that I'm being bullied it will put me outside the group
- if I intervene I might be bullied too
- if I tell someone, how do I know that I will be taken seriously?

- my experience tells me that the bully will get me no matter what I do.

The bullying behaviour that had been described was clearly working against the ethos of Special Needs at Salisbury College. As challenging behaviour of this kind, taking place inside or outside the classroom, can prevent learning from taking place and affect the atmosphere in which we work, the problem belonged not only to those who were being bullied but to all of us. The bullies within the group had targeted particular students but in doing so had created problems that could affect the well-being of all: individual students no longer had sole ownership of the problems.

Collective responsibility had dispelled their fear of reprisals and had allowed the discussion to move forward. Incidents that had been recurring throughout the term were described; the bullies were identified by members of the group, and named. With no more secrecy to hide behind, their behaviour was confronted by their fellow students in an open and direct manner. The bullies were required to acknowledge and 'own' their behaviour and take responsibility for the damage and distress they had caused.

It has since been suggested that a session of this kind could become a lynch mob, but within the democratic structure of the discussion those who had bullied were given the same opportunities as those who had been bullied, with students who had not been involved in either behaviour playing a mediating role. This format (which is a student council rather than a bully court) aims at perceived justice and reparation rather than retribution and punishment. The desired outcomes, agreed by the group, are very specific: that the bully makes good any damage he/she has caused and that a change in behaviour is seen to take place.

Within this structure a student who had witnessed the harassment of another over a long period of time, without finding the courage to speak out was, at last, able to say:

> You took David's cigarettes and kicked him. You've been waiting for him to get off the bus and following him all the way to College calling him names and pushing him in the back. You had money for your own cigarettes. Why did you have to do this?

The discussion established that the bullies did not have to do this ... they had chosen to behave in this way. Being responsible for what we do, thinking about what we say and recognising its effects, and acknowledging that we have a choice are all part of the transition into young adulthood that many young people with Special Needs find difficult to cope with. Emphasising the notion of choice in relation to bullying behaviour helped us to overcome blocking strategies (e.g. 'Why did you do this?'... 'I don't know') and enabled the group to hand back the behaviour and its problems to the bullies making it very clear that such behaviour was not acceptable to any of us, under any circumstances.

Labelling the behaviour more specifically also enabled members of staff to underline the seriousness of bullying incidents:

> 'When you stole David's cigarettes...'
> *'We didn't steal them, we just took them.'*
> 'If David didn't want you to take them it was stealing.'
> *'It was only cigarettes.'*
> 'If you take something that doesn't belong to you without the owner's permission it's stealing... you are a thief. If you try to frighten David into giving you the cigarettes by threatening him or hitting him it's called robbery, and that's against the law.'

Behaviour that had been accepted as part of childhood experience now had legal implications. These young people required information about their rights and responsibilities according to the law.

Shifting the balance of power within the group away from the bullies started by exposing their behaviour in this way. They could no longer rely on secrecy and threats to maintain control of others. Giving the group appropriate skills, support and the opportunity to assume responsibility for solving their own problems had redistributed power in a very effective way.

Communication skills and problem solving at a level commensurate with each student's ability forms part of the core curriculum and now gives emphasis to Assertiveness training which includes: open and direct communication, saying 'No', receiving and giving criticism, dealing with conflict, coping with a put-down, dealing with anger, and the use of correct words to influence people. Building confidence and body awareness, being able to stand tall and look someone in the eye, gaining a good self image with respect for oneself and others can effect important changes in behaviour. Role play, drama, puppet theatre, creative studies and project work can help a young person with learning difficulties to practise these skills, with personal presentation, hairdressing and beauty therapy playing an important part in building a good self image and a sense of well-being. Acquiring and putting into practice powerful communication skills enhanced self esteem and prepared the way for this group of students to begin to take responsibility for solving their own problems. Many had learned from their own experience that even if a parent or a teacher sought to alleviate the problems that bullying presents there will come a time when the bully will take his chances and the victim will find himself in the wrong place at the wrong time. In fact many young people have told me they feel that parental intervention could only make matters worse. Empowering students with appropriate skills, providing a supportive network, and establishing a format for confronting the issues as they occur enabled students to feel that they could attend their College classes in safety.

In attempting to find their own solutions the students agreed that:

○ Salisbury College of Technology would discount 'tale telling'; and any behaviour calculated to cause distress, pain or discomfort to another person, or wilful damage to his or her possessions would be reported to a member of staff.
○ Bullying behaviour would be discussed with the student council as soon after the incident as possible.
○ A written account of any bullying behaviour would be made by each of the participants and would be signed, dated and witnessed and kept as part of that person's records for a specified period of time.
○ Parents would be informed of the behaviour without delay and would receive a copy of the statements.
○ The student council together with staff and parents would agree appropriate sanctions to remedy the situation.
○ If the behaviour could not be resolved in this way the matter would be referred to the Head of Faculty.
○ Any person witnessing a bullying incident without doing something about it would be held equally responsible.

To support these strategies it was necessary to look at ways in which the College environment could be made less conducive to bullying incidents and this proved to be very difficult as students are, at any one time, likely to be in several different parts of the campus. As we could do little to change the environment we looked for ways of lessening the opportunities for a potential bully. These were mainly centred around the lunch break when students with Special Needs together with mainstream students attended the refectory, and afterwards, during the time before classes recommenced in the afternoon.

To alleviate this, two Care Assistants have been timetabled to accompany students, on an informal basis, to have lunch at the refectory, to share this time as a social occasion, to act as befrienders and confidants, to initiate conversation and assist students to integrate with others in an acceptable way. In doing this they have been able to pinpoint attitudes and problem areas which might be occurring between students, and pass on this information to the Tutor/ Organiser for discussion at staff meetings. It has also enabled them to help those students who were on the periphery of the group, for one reason or another, to interact with others in a more relaxed and constructive way. It was important to ensure that students were not made to feel that they were being supervised because they could not be trusted, and the notion of sharing a social time with a particular member of staff has been fostered.

On two days a week, as part of a domestic skills session, different groups of students now plan and prepare lunch at the study base to which other students and staff are invited. This not only gives an opportunity to practise problem solving, planning, organising, numeracy, communication skills and a variety of practical skills, but also presents a wide area of endeavour within which individual students may experience success. International cookery incorporating dishes from Greece, Turkey, America, China and India, as well as the more traditional regional dishes from our own country have stimulated interest. In line with a more constructive approach to leisure time, optional activities such as disco dancing classes are now organised by the students, and quiet areas have been designated for those who want to read or have a chat. In order to provide a further leisure option, the study base garden has been turfed and students have built a barbecue and garden furniture with funds they have raised themselves. They have also built and stocked an outdoor aviary. A Lunch Club has been established giving students the opportunity to organise a variety of activities including board game tournaments.

Mainstream students studying the Performing Arts have contributed to the activities by organising expressive movement sessions and short drama projects, and a student from the adjoining College of Art and Design has, as part of her Foundation Course, encouraged students with learning difficulties to take part in activities using a variety of art materials. In this way mainstream students and students with learning difficulties are able, with the support of staff, to give as well as gain from each other. Working together, in co-operation rather than competition, these young people are encouraged to recognise and value each others' strengths and support each others' weaknesses in order to complete a project or get a job done. This is not always easy (particularly for students who have behavioural problems of one kind or another) but personality clashes and day to day conflicts, which do not necessarily constitute bullying, are dealt with as they occur by the students themselves, or with the intervention of a member of staff. This broad base of student activities and interests also gives opportunities for realistic sanctions on unacceptable behaviour.

In order to minimise opportunities for unacceptable behaviour when students are changing classrooms or moving about the College, timetabling has been reassessed and now provides little time for dawdling or messing about. When leaving a classroom or workshop attention is drawn to the time and students are reminded that someone is waiting for them: 'It's quarter past ten and Mr Hibberd is waiting for you'. It is, therefore, very important that Tutors are in the classrooms or workshops before the students arrive so that groups are not left waiting, unsupervised, either inside the classroom or in the corridors. To encourage an awareness of time and punctuality students are required, on arriving at College, to clock-in with an individual weekly clock card at a machine located at the study base, and to clock-out whenever they leave the campus. This also gives practice in a work-related skill and underlines expectations of responsible behaviour. Lockers have been provided for personal possessions and the keys are kept in a key press at the study base. Students have access to their keys on request and are responsible for keeping their own things safe. Bags, lunch packets and other personal belongings left lying about the cloakroom are confiscated; students remind each other of this and in this way the premises are kept tidy and secure.

Establishing standards begins at Induction when each new entrant is given a 'College friend', i.e. a student who is willing to act as a guide to help the new person to settle in and find his/her way about the campus. A responsible student may have two or even three 'freshers' under his wing, giving him status and building confidence. This also enables new students to be integrated into the group more effectively and the network of relationships is strengthened by this support. New students do not leave established behaviours behind on entering Further Education and each new intake may include students who have bullied in the past. Since they are eager to create a place for themselves within a new situation, unacceptable dominant behaviour may emerge. Quick action to deal with this, combined with a comprehensive Induction programme, can clear the way for making a good transition from school to College and acceptable standards of behaviour can be reinforced.

These strategies have helped to provide the framework within which we have begun to address the issues of bullying as they have affected students with moderate learning difficulties whilst on the College campus, but the problem does not end there. Off campus bullying by students towards one another can be reported and dealt with by using the strategies described, but bullying by other people off the campus required more than enhanced communication skills and assertiveness. We needed further information and support and found it when we contacted our local Community Policeman who now visits us regularly. His information and advice has supported the work we are doing and has enabled us to act in an advisory capacity to parents who are having to deal with the problems of bullying. In doing this it is necessary to define the terms very clearly so that individual rights and responsibilities are understood. For example: a child under the age of ten years cannot commit a crime. Serious matters, however, should be brought to the attention of the authorities as action can sometimes be taken. A child aged ten to sixteen years is a juvenile and must be dealt with by the Police and Courts in a special way; Magistrates do have powers to enforce their wishes, and teachers are supported when evidence is presented to the Court. Upon their seventeenth birthday the full sanction of the law is available for all offences, and the child becomes an adult for all criminal law purposes. This includes aspects of bullying behaviours which can be described as common assault, the more serious offence of criminal assault, and threatening behaviour. Damage to clothing or other personal effects, whether or not the damage was intended, can amount to criminal damage and constitute an arrestable offence in which the bully need only be reckless.

Providing information, acting as a liaison between worried parents and the police, and providing a supportive atmosphere in which problems of this kind can be addressed not only enables us to look after the best interest of our students, but also helps to alleviate, by positive action, some of the feelings of helplessness and anger that victims and their parents may experience. It is important that Senior Managers are kept informed of circumstances requiring this kind of informal advisory support.

Salisbury College of Technology has an important dynamic role within the community and Senior Management acknowledge and support the contribution made by Special Needs students and staff. It has taken up the issues of bullying in a very positive way with conferences, seminars and workshops aimed at disseminating information and skills to colleges, schools and other agencies. Assertion Training classes and workshops are available to give teachers, parents and children the means by which they may start to make changes. Changing behaviour, however, is not easy and dealing with some situations will take practice. Ascertaining that bullying is actually taking place needs careful handling: the bully, in spite of certain common characteristics, is not always easy to detect, and is often incapable of changing his behaviour without help. It is important that all the people involved are aware of the rules and that they combine to ensure that the rules are adhered to: dealing with bullying is, in our experience, a collective responsibility requiring a high degree of vigilance and cross college support.

Secure within a framework of shared responsibility, students with Special Education Needs at the Salisbury College of Technology now speak out against physical and verbal bullying. Personal tutors are designated to give advice and help to put problems into perspective, and where necessary bring them to the attention of the student council. If a meeting is agreed, all the students on that particular course are obliged to attend and the Tutor/Organiser, with other members of staff, acts as a facilitator.

These strategies, based on effective communication skills, mutual support and good community relations have worked for us. They have shown us that a willingness to confront the issues of bullying can empower students who have learning difficulties, and enable them to empower each other. These young people, despite a variety of handicaps or disabilities, have the same expectations of life as any other group of students who are making the transition into young adulthood. Like any other group of young people they have the right to be able to attend College and go about their day to day business in safety.

CHAPTER 6

The Heartstone Odyssey: *Exploring the Heart of Bullying*

Angela M. Horton

Imagine a railway carriage. The scene is tense. A young dancer of Indian origin, accompanied by eight mouse friends, watches with horror as two white British men threaten to beat up a ticket inspector. Why? Because he looks Asian. Because he asked the men for their tickets. Because he had requested them to remove their feet from the seats.

> One of the men reached up and grabbed the inspector's jacket, pulling him down. 'I told you Paki, we don't take orders from your kind.' . . . Snuggletoes (the youngest mouse) could stand it no longer. Perhaps he hadn't been on adventures before, but he wasn't going to sit and watch this. With one jump he was off the table, across the carriage, and beside the old lady. 'Can I borrow one of your pencils please?' he said. 'Of course', whispered the old lady, 'but be careful'. 'No', said Snuggletoes, he'd seen enough of being careful . . . Snuggletoes took a big scoop of ice cream from the tub and balanced a spoon across the pencil like a see-saw. Then he climbed up on to the edge of the tub and jumped down, stamping on the end of the spoon as he landed. The ice cream flew through the air and hit the man straight in the face. He jumped back in surprise and let go of the ticket inspector . . . 'Vermin, I'll get you for that' said the man, 'and your Paki friends' . . . The two men got up and began to lurch down the carriage . . . 'What's all this!' a huge voice boomed from the end of the carriage . . . There . . . stood the guard, one of the largest men any of them had ever seen. 'Right you two, down in the guards' van with me and you get off at the next stop. Now move!'

Dramatic and direct, *The Heartstone Odyssey* was born on 26th March, 1985. That night, a train pulled out of Central Station in Bombay and headed out into the dark towards the foothills of the Western Ghats mountains of Maharashtra State in India. On board was a storyteller, Arvan Kumar, who entertained his fellow passengers by telling them the tale of the Heartstone.

It is this story which has so excited parents, teachers, professional groups of various kinds and – most importantly – a host of children that the book is about to be reprinted for the fourth time and has already sold 9,000 copies.

Why the excitement? Bullying amongst children is increasingly recognised as a major problem and one which is far more widespread than often realised. Racist behaviour among adults is also clearly visible across Britain. Through the characters and events in the story, the book supports and helps children who have been bullied or suffered prejudice for any reason. It also provides more fortunate children with deeper insights into relationships with others and encourages them to develop sympathetic and understanding attitudes.

Although the book is lengthy, reflecting the oral traditions of India, yet it holds the attention of children aged seven to eleven years, fascinating them with its mixture of the real and imaginary.

Through this secondary world of caring mice and evil crows, presided over by the Spirit of the Land in the form of an elephant, children are invited to discuss painful and difficult issues which continue to perplex the adult world. They are encouraged to speak openly about how these ideas relate to their own lives. In this way, the book helps adults and children to step across the boundaries of age, gender, background, beliefs, cultures, race, illness and disability, thus destroying the segregation from which stem so many fears and falsehoods that lead to prejudice and bullying.

The Heartstone Odyssey has been successfully used by infant and primary schools in every part of Britain, in all-white areas, in those where ninety-nine per cent of the population is Asian and those where a mix of races live alongside each other. It has also been used by the School of Education at the University of Exeter to help raise awareness of issues related to multicultural education in initial teacher training for undergraduates.

A fundamental part of exploring *The Heartstone Odyssey* and the issues of prejudice and bullying is to set up a Story Circle. In order to do this, groups of children (it is best not to have more than thirty) meet regularly with an adult (not necessarily a teacher) perhaps at lunch time or after school. The adult begins to read the book, as it is written, despite its length. Experience has shown that editing is unnecessary for any but the very youngest children – and even then, many schools report that they can read the *Odyssey* in its entirety. During Story Circle time, children discuss the tale and the issues raised, relating them to the real world and their own lives. Although, at its core, the Heartstone story is about racial prejudice and harassment, in practice it has created a forum in which victims of many different kinds of bullying may speak.

It is not difficult to qualify as a sympathetic adult with whom the children can explore in this way. Any teacher, community worker, parent, relative or friend can help. The only requirement is for the children to respect that adult such that they can listen in a disciplined way. Any adult helper needs to read the story first and to feel comfortable with it. Naturally, the Story Circle leader will purchase a copy of the book, but apart from this, no other resources are necessary in order to get started on a small scale.

It would seem perfectly reasonable to enquire whether there has been any feedback from the schools. Indeed there has – quite a lot! In the first place, several schools have reported that an atmosphere of trust has been build up between staff and children who then feel it is 'safe' to talk. There is also an acceptance by the children that even adults are not infallible, and may have suffered harassment themselves. Within this framework, incidents of harassment and bullying that take place both in and outside school have come to light. Moreover, involving parents from different communities at various levels of Heartstone work has led to increased respect for those communities.

But the most exciting reports concern the way that children develop their *own* ideas about how to stop harassment and bullying in their world. Children have been observed in playgrounds making a stand against the bullies instead of looking the other way and ignoring unpleasant incidents. Some children have lobbied their local town council to remove racist graffiti from public walls. Others have drawn up a 'Charter for the People', in which they make a commitment themselves towards striving against bullying and prejudice and call for others to do the same. Name-calling and the like are out!

Another interesting development has been the way children have begun to question things which they had previously taken for granted. The concept of one group believing itself to be 'right' above all others and the evils to which this can lead has been challenged in many places.

Role-play based on characters and episodes in the book has helped real-life victims to develop assertiveness and given bullies a strong message to change their ways. Role-play sessions have often led to acting out incidents experienced by real individuals and, in this way, practical methods of coping with such incidents have been devised by the children. Youngsters from minority groups of all kinds, ranging from travellers' children to disabled children, and those from Asian, Afro-Caribbean, Eastern European and Jewish cultures, to name but a few, have been found to blossom as a result of Heartstone work. In particular, Asian girls have been seen to develop a sense of pride in themselves. Modelling themselves on the Indian dancer/heroine, Chandra, in the story, they come to speculate that perhaps they too may have their achievements recognised.

In order to ensure that each Story Circle never runs out of material or ideas, and in order to provide an instrument by which groups may keep in touch with one another, a monthly magazine called *Stonekeeper* was created. The story told in *The Heartstone Odyssey* is continued in a second book, *India and Beyond*. This is being serialised in *Stonekeeper*, but there is also much more within its covers. There are feature articles on the themes of different people, the natural world and history. There are practical suggestions for projects and access to all leaders of other Story Circles who have contributed their ideas. In this way, both children and adults can feel part of a network working for change; one which values their own ideas for influencing their immediate world, both socially and environmentally. It is interesting to note how much material written by children is included in *Stonekeeper* and that children with low self-esteem are particularly enthusiastic about making a contribution.

One important development for *Stonekeeper* is that the general background features, providing information about temples, countries, animals, and so on, will soon be transferred to large, full-colour wall charts and distributed free, as part of the subscription. Future plans also provide for the number of features on bullying, prejudice, and story-telling traditions to be increased.

Libraries, play schemes, community groups and other centres which can provide facilities for story-telling have become involved as Story Circles in addition to schools.

If you want to start two school Story Circle groups from scratch (including the need to catch up on what has been written already, as well as stay abreast of mouse news) here is what you would need to purchase:

Story Update Pack (*India and Beyond*)	£11.50
One year's subscription to *Stonekeeper*	£40.00
Two copies of *The Heartstone Odyssey*	£10.00
	£61.50

Another exciting evolution in Heartstone work is that which is being developed by an Indian contemporary dancer named Sitakumari. A friend and colleague of author, Arvan Kumar, Sita is able to visit schools in order to tell parts of the story and, more importantly, to dance and mime parts of the *Odyssey* using traditional Indian stylised movements. Children take part in the miming and dancing at every opportunity. In some cases, major performances involving hundreds of children have taken place, for example in Birmingham Cathedral in February 1990. It was a stirring sight!

Acting out parts of *The Heartstone Odyssey* often connects up very conveniently with work done under the national curriculum. Science, English, Geography, History and RE take up many aspects of the Heartstone story, which also acts as a springboard for work related to cross-curricular dimensions and themes such as environmental education, economic awareness, the world of work, citizenship, health education, and multicultural education. A Heartstone Education Pack has been published in order to support teachers with ideas for activities in different parts of the curriculum, and is being continuously updated and extended.

The Heartstone team would like to extend their work in a meaningful way, based on the evaluation of people in many parts of the total community. R. A. German, Principal Education Officer of the Commission for Racial Equality, commented in November 1988:

> *The Heartstone Odyssey* confronts what we sometimes call the real world with magic, mystery, danger and rescue, suspense and resolution in the most gripping and entertaining way...it echoes the heartfelt needs of children for a world that assures them of justice, equality, freedom and respect. I want every school in the land to introduce its children to this story, which is one of the finest I have ever read.

The Rt. Hon. Tony Benn MP had this to say:

> I am deeply impressed by what has been achieved in getting across a message of hope in a way that touches on some of the central problems of our society without endangering the project by provoking a hostile backlash.

Evaluations of Heartstone projects across the country have been carried out by a variety of people seeking information in order to decide whether to provide financial support to the Heartstone team. National funding of Heartstone projects is considerable. Camden, Derbyshire, Crawley, Ealing, Havering, Hounslow, Islington, Kingston-upon-Thames, Newham, Richmond and Wandsworth Borough Councils have supported the work. Birmingham Education Authority, Barnet Education Department, Manchester Education Committee, Sutton Education Department, together with Basildon Council, Watford County Council, Westminster City Council, West Midlands Arts Association, East Midlands Arts Association, North-West Arts Association have all provided funds. Assistance has also been received through the Home Office Safer Cities programme, the Department of the Environment through the Inner Area Programme, the Paul Hamlyn Foundation, the Metropolitan Police and Sheffield Police.

From this, it is clear that *The Heartstone Odyssey* is highly regarded by many people. This is not to say, of course, that some people do not experience initial qualms in undertaking Heartstone activities. Some teachers have been worried about not being able to handle what comes up in discussion. However, in reality, almost all teachers do cope, and cope well, with points raised in conversation. In any event, the Heartstone team are constantly ready to support any person who might feel anxious about handling certain issues, and people are always welcome to contact them about any concerns they may have. Within this context, it is interesting to note that the incidents talked about are commonplace for many minority groups. Far from being upset by them, these groups are only too happy to bring their experiences to the surface and to discover that they are 'among friends'.

A few adults have been worried that the story is too long. Nevertheless, in practice, this has not generally been found to be true. Indeed, far better responses have been reported from places where the story was not edited down. Naturally, no story can please all children. However, of those children who have heard the tale, there have been few who have not enjoyed a major part of it. On the rare occasions when enjoyment was absent there has appeared to be more than one reason for this, often relating to matters of a social/emotional nature.

Another worry has been that working with *The Heartstone Odyssey* might put certain families from minority groups at risk. This has not happened. In practice, in one example a group of children were able to speak openly of threats they were receiving at home (prior to any work on Heartstone starting in their school). As a result of this, the school went to support and aid the family.

Similarly, fears have been expressed that *The Heartstone Odyssey* might actually initiate name-calling where none existed before. This has not happened yet. In one minor incident recently, a group of children took up the word 'Paki', mistakenly believing that because their teacher had uttered the word, it was all right for them to now use it openly – it was already a word that was commonly used by them when not in the company of adults. However, the teacher was able to explain to the children how important it was not to hurt people by using the word, and this idea was further reinforced by continued reading of the story.

Using the book with children aged twelve or more is not always successful, since youngsters at this age are beginning to lose interest in 'childish' representations of things. Having said that, however, there are some Story Circles whose members are of secondary school age. These young people have looked at the issues raised in relation to the diary of Anne Frank and the life of Martin Luther King.

It is important not to rush the reading of the Heartstone story so that time can be given for thoughts and ideas to be voiced and where necessary, challenged. Assimilation of new ideas leading to change in attitude and behaviour does take time, hence the Story Circle concept of a regular small slot each week so that the children come to recognise it as the period in which they will be able to speak of their feelings openly and without fear.

So what does the future hold for *The Heartstone Odyssey*? Well, it certainly looks as though the message concerning prejudice and bullying will travel further afield. Already, steps have been taken to encourage children to read the book in Malawi, Canada, India and Japan. It may be that Dr S. Bakshi, who is the Medical Officer for Environmental Health on Birmingham City Council, most clearly sums up the role of *The Heartstone Odyssey* when he says:

> Hearts and minds are not won by laws and shouting about rights. That way lies confrontation. Live and let live may be a good policy in a prison camp, but living with each other in harmony and love will only come about by making outsiders feel insiders. The (Heartstone) story...is a moving one, the narrative spellbinding. No person who reads it will ever be the same again...

Further information about *The Heartstone Odyssey* may be obtained from: Allied Mouse Ltd., 1st Floor, Longden Court, Spring Gardens,

Buxton, Derbyshire, SK17 6BZ. Hopefully, many other youngsters will engage with the Heartstone in the years to come, and nothing will ever be the same again for them. We look forward to a world without any kind of bullying.

CHAPTER 7

A Practical Approach through Drama and Workshops

Francis Gobey

Only Playing, Miss is the Neti-Neti Theatre Company's play about bullying. Written by Penny Casdagli, with additional songs by Caroline Griffin, it is performed multilingually in English, Sign Language and Bengali. Initially it played to junior secondary school audiences of deaf and hearing young people, but has since also been performed to general adult theatre audiences.

It tells the story of Eugene Hickey, returning to his class after the death of his father, whose behaviour is seen by some of his classmates as out of order. David Rant begins to bully him – joined by Sam, who turns her friends against Becky, Eugene's ally. The bullying intensifies, despite the efforts of Eugene's friend Jo, until Becky decides to tell their teacher. Mrs Richards confronts the bullies, and contacts the parents. Eugene then finds the courage to stand up to David Rant, and Rant to share the story of his own bereavement with Eugene.

This story, presented in colloquial dialogue and song, is readily accessible to the school audience. It is understood that the loss of a parent stands for all the vulnerabilities that bullying takes advantage of. It offers no easy solutions, but uses the real-life nature of the story to make an impact and all the resources of drama to break the silence which bullying relies on. In this it is helped by Neti-Neti's performance practice.

The Neti-Neti Theatre Company

Neti-Neti is a Zen Buddhist term meaning 'not this, not that', suggesting an idea of perfect harmony. Founded in 1987, the Neti-Neti Theatre Company is co-directed by Penny Casdagli and Caroline Griffin, who also teaches in a boys' comprehensive school in London. It aims to produce high quality drama, relevant to young people as well as to adults, and supported by published material and practical education work. The emphasis is on exploring language, communication and the experience and perceptions of disability, particularly hidden disability.

All performances are presented multilingually (often in English, Sign Language and Bengali) by a fully integrated cast of differently-abled actors. Neti-Neti's equal opportunity policy covers hidden disability and sexual orientation as well as race, gender and disability. With black, Asian and deaf performers playing substantially positive roles, *Only Playing, Miss* implicitly challenges racist and ablist attitudes – especially important for Neti-Neti's constituencies of deaf and Bengali-speaking young people.

The origins of the project

The idea was suggested to Penny Casdagli by the suffering of a young friend, who was being bullied at her primary school. As a playwright, Penny responded with a play. She developed a workshop version with student actors in the Guildhall School of Music and Drama, but the response from the schools they worked in quickly convinced Caroline Griffin and her that *Only Playing, Miss* should be more deeply researched, rewritten multilingually, and taken forward into a fully professional production.

It was as a part of this process that I was employed, with funding from the Sir John Cass Foundation, as Neti-Neti's Education Officer. I ran an initial series of writing workshops in ten London secondary schools to find out how bullying affected 11 to 13 year-olds, and what they thought could be done about it. Selections from their writings were published, along with the script, in the programme which accompanied performances of *Only Playing, Miss* on an eight-week tour in 1989.

One of these workshops and some extracts from the play were featured on BBC2's 'Forty Minutes' documentary called *Bullies* (November 1989). By the start of 1990, Neti-Neti had received hundreds of enquiries about the play and workshops from schools, LEAs, educational psychologists, researchers, writers, teachers, parents and victims of bullying. It was therefore decided to revive the play as soon as possible – which in the current funding climate turned out to be Autumn 1990 – and to make a professional broadcast-quality video of *Only Playing, Miss* for schools and institutions unable to see – or wanting to follow up – a performance. Both these were done.

Such was the interest in Neti-Neti's workshop approach that I was able to continue and develop my educational work in 1990. Without the immediate goal of making a written contribution to the programme booklet, the workshops concentrated more on

- **using drama as a means of approaching the problem of bullying.**
  They also became a way of
- **supporting schools and LEAs in their anti-bullying initiatives,** as detailed in the rest of this chapter.

I have gone into this history in some detail because I think the growth of a project is as important as its fruits, especially with a 'hidden subject' such as bullying. The initial work began in Penny Casdagli and Caroline Griffin's response to someone suffering the pain of being bullied. It was out of this that *Only Playing, Miss* and everything associated with it grew.

Neti-Neti's subsequent work has coincided with the coming out of bullying as an academic, media and educational issue, but when I now talk about whole-school policies, LEA initiatives and intervention strategies, I remember how it began. This is also how the drama works – in the simple, fruitful act of empathy.

Why workshops?

In industry a workshop is a place of trial and error, of experiment with prototypes. It is also the place where ways of doing things are put under as much scrutiny as what is done.

In school a Neti-Neti workshop is not the same as a class. It is:

- ○ run by someone from outside the school.
- ○ mysterious – no-one says the first one is *about* bullying.
- ○ one of a series of 2 or 3, usually leading up to a play.
- ○ smaller – one leader works with 15–18 children.
- ○ in the presence of a teacher not being 'the teacher'.
- ○ often a cross-section of pupils from different classes.

By being active, participatory and co-operative, the workshop sets up its own social dynamic which aims to give equal space to each individual and promote group cohesion. It also lets no-one off the hook: at times an individual might need to be on their own, but most of the exercises are built without a back seat.

The basic structure and starting point of the workshop is a circle. A circle is safe in that no-one can do things behind your back, but challenging in that it exposes you to everyone else's gaze. In fact all the exercises operate on this principle, offering the protection of a dramatic *role* to the honest expression of vulnerable feeling and belief.

I explain and demonstrate but do very little talking in my roles as organiser, participant, observer, camera-operator, interviewer and random donor of role-cards. I do not want a teacher–class dynamic because that would be usurping the potential of the workshop's own ethos. This is important because it is making a strong implicit statement against bullying behaviour.

Why drama?

Bullying lies within the range of normal social behaviour encountered by most children. They know what it is and who does it – though few admit to doing it themselves. A class discussion rarely gets much further than that: some people are bullies, some are victims, some are neither, that is the way things are.

Drama can help to extend and deepen an agreed definition of bullying. In the first workshop I use a series of mimed 'give-us-a-clue' role plays to illustrate a variety of one-to-one situations. These include the use and abuse of power at school and in the family, persuasion tactics, teasing, name-calling, excluding, and physical bullying. To make it easier for pupils to recognise these for what they are, I start the workshop with intensive mime work on feelings and expressing feelings. A teasing remark looks on the surface quite different from a blow to the head, but if the intention of the bully and the hurt feelings of the victim are fully expressed, those watching will grant that they are similar.

Drama can also help establish that behaviour is to a certain extent a matter of choice and personal responsibility. Just as an actor tries out a role, so can workshop participants try out different sorts of behaviour. I sometimes arrange it that quiet pupils get the more confident roles, or that demanding ones have to act against type. By acting out and examining roles (more or less randomly) assigned, the group demonstrates that it is the behaviour of the bully which is the problem, not their existence. Also, it is seen that a change in behaviour on the part of the whole group (including the victim) might in turn affect the bully's behaviour. Later I make this clearer by involving everyone as 'friends' in the decision-making of the role-characters, as in this improvised dilemma of the bully's friend:

> Me: *I wonder if I should tell the teacher. Michael's probably my best friend. I don't know what to do. What shall I do?*
> A1: Go and tell.
> A2: Nah, don't tell. He might beat you up.
> Me: *I could have him at any time. I don't know why I should be scared of him.*
> A1: You shouldn't be scared of anyone, see. Stand up to bullies.
> A2: I don't think you can beat him up.
> Me: *It doesn't matter if I can't beat him up. If I go to the teacher, he'll sort him out quickly.*
> A1: Yes that's true. Teachers can always do things.
> Me: *I don't know what to do.*
> A2: It's up to you.
> Me: *I'm going to tell. That's it.*

How does this help the pupils?

The participants in the workshop go through a series of structured games, exercises, improvisations and discussions designed to make the process fun as well as challenging. The exact shape of the workshop depends on how many I am doing in one school, and if more than one, how long a gap there is before the next. I prefer to do at least two workshops with the same pupils and to spend at least $1\frac{1}{2}$ hours with them each time.

The justification for working with such a small group is that the useful work which is done can then be passed on to the whole year-group. Considering how difficult it is for schools, LEAs (and theatre companies) to get money for extra-curricular work, my best bet lies with achieving something quick, concentrated and concrete in the time available, and with making my workshop a pilot, not a one-off project. This is done by involving other pupils in a questionnaire survey, and by making a record of the workshop in writing, on display boards, on tape and on video – this documentation being, in fact, part of the workshop process.

In one Derbyshire school the second workshop was structured

around questionnaires which the group had helped to compile themselves. These were about types of behaviour, incidents of bullying or being bullied, feelings/friends/enemies, and the use/abuse of power. In the break, pairs took clipboards out into the playground and interviewed their fellow students. Among the questions the students themselves added were:

> Have you ever been called racist names?
> How do you feel when someone cusses you or your family?
> Have you ever been bullied by a *popular* person?
> Have you ever picked on someone about their weight?
> If you were teasing someone, how would you know when to stop?

This was not intended to be a full survey, which could be done later. It did, however, spread the word that bullying was being looked into, in anticipation of the upcoming performance of *Only Playing, Miss*. Excitement was added by the presence of a camera, and interesting stories were taped. These were mainly remembered rather than actual, as I suspect will always be the case in such circumstances. Finally the survey gave the workshop some rough data for subsequent work: on differences between boys' and girls' experiences of bullying, on the occurrence of racist or sexist remarks in the playground, on what excuses were made for making someone a victim.

The group went on to make a video of what it felt like to be involved in a bullying situation (as bully, victim, friend, onlooker, parent or teacher), and how a particular problem might be solved. I use a structure of 'dilemma' decision-making in which the choice made determines the next improvisation: for instance, a witness of bullying might choose to tell a friend, a parent might choose to see the teacher. The 'solution' is thus a gradual process of negotiation.

Their final goal was to produce a display for the corridor, collating their written and graphic work into a *Help and Advice Poster*. This included:

- **Advice for the victim** – Tell a friend or trusted teacher; Don't stay off school; Try to walk away from the bully, don't run . . .
- **Ideas on how to help the bully** – Talk to them; Help them understand how others feel. Suspend them . . .
- **Suggestions for preventative measures and school policy** – Talk to the parents; Have a room people can go to for help . . .

Students in another school had this advice to add:

> If you are getting bullied by a teacher, you should write it down, and

tell your friends to write it down as well, so you have evidence. If one teacher doesn't believe you, you should try another one.

And this:

If you get it out in the open, you've got more chance of solving it.

How does it help the school?

A teacher is always present during the workshop, either as observer or participant. I have gone through the plan with them beforehand and will have a meeting on follow-up work afterwards.

A West London school offers the ideal scenario: The Deputy Head is concerned over 'cussing' and harassment in the playground. She hears of Neti-Neti's work, *Only Playing, Miss* and my workshops. The Head of PSE and pastoral tutors are keen. She books the play, finds the money, and arranges a meeting with me. As a result I run two afternoon sessions with the pastoral staff. The first leads them through some of the workshop exercises to reawaken the painful feelings involved, and explains the rationale behind using drama in this sort of work. Some of the teachers are not used to role-play and some find that it brings back uncomfortable memories of their own schooldays.

One simple exercise illustrates this. Two people face each other close up: one of them can only say YES, the other can only say NO. For thirty seconds they argue, each trying to make their position prevail. Some pairs rapidly escalated into shouting matches, others (my own included) duelled with icy pianissimos. Afterwards I asked them to detail the feelings that the game aroused in them, and what they thought the argument could have been about. In the workshops themselves I have tied this exercise in with resisting-bullying work, and also used it as a before and after game to show how assertiveness can come with practice.

The second session is a more open, teacher-centred discussion of anti-bullying strategies and whole-school policy. There are two sides to this. First, what agreed guidelines to follow in a discovered case of serious bullying. Second, and more difficult, how to create a school or class ethos in which bullying behaviour rarely happens in the first place. My particular expertise lies in the use of drama, but I am aware of a wide range of approaches which I also put on the agenda of this session: behaviour contracts, Kidscape programmes, honour courts, cross-curriculum and PSE models.

Later I return with a colleague and, with the help of these and other teachers (and a few interested sixth formers), do eight extended workshops over two days with second year groups. We produce videos, advice packs, written and taped stories, questionnaires and drawings. The entire year-group subsequently sees the play.

It is up to each school what further use they make of Neti-Neti's work. In this case the teachers involved said that they appreciated the different relationship with the pupils that the workshops gave, and would try to do similar work with other classes. The Deputy Head and PSE department wanted to take up some of the workshop techniques and materials and incorporate them in a 'bullying' unit on the lower school PSE curriculum.

Trentham Books' *'Only Playing, Miss': playscript/workshops* (see footnote), in which I give an account of the workshops, will be very useful to them here, as will the video of *Only Playing, Miss* and schools playscripts published by Neti-Neti (see footnote). These will enable the anti-bullying work to continue as the company moves on to new projects and new plays.

How does it help the Local Education Authority?

In some instances it has been the Education Authority which has taken the initiative to promote Neti-Neti's work in schools. They have not just paid for performances and workshops, but taken the opportunity to make bullying an Authority-wide issue, involving Heads, Inspectors and policy-makers.

Neti-Neti has especially good links with our own borough of Islington. Their LEA's dynamic new Equal Opportunities Inspector included our work in the 1990 INSET Training schedule, and we were contracted to run workshops and perform *Only Playing, Miss* in all eight Islington secondary schools. An anti-harassment statement is being prepared by her Equal Opportunities team, building on the work of ILEA, and Neti-Neti's anti-bullying work is seen as a useful contribution.

Close involvement of Heads (some of whom popped into the workshops) and of the Drama, English or PSE staff I worked with, ensured that the workshops, the play and the issues they raised can be taken up by the whole school. As before, the actual impact of the performance and workshops can also be extended by using Neti-Neti's questionnaire, book, playscripts and video in follow-up work.

Another feature of Neti-Neti's cooperation with Islington is the approach to the Company made by the Schools Liaison Service of the police. They were informed of our work and came to a performance of *Only Playing, Miss* in a local school. Their present educational campaign deals with street robbery and 'joeys' – youngsters who are bullied into committing crimes – and the lessons they use contain units on self-assertiveness and knowing your rights. They were keen to find out how drama could help. They said the performance had given them some ideas.

Conclusion

Only Playing, Miss is only a play. The Neti-Neti Theatre Company doesn't on its own have the answers to a school's bullying problem. The hope in Islington, and in every school that we go to, is that the initiatives we set up can 'cascade' through, so that each school is enabled to do the comprehensive groundwork needed to make equal opportunities a reality.

Because if there is one thing we've learnt from performing *Only Playing, Miss* and running workshops in schools it is this: the play is a young people's production dealing with issues that are part and parcel of being a young person in a school today – and as such it is very warmly received everywhere we go. But the crucial response, which decides what happens thereafter, is the response of the adults present.

We noticed this at the first evening performance, when the adult audience reacted to the play in a way profoundly different from the afternoon's young people. For them the painful feelings associated with bullying, whether suffered or witnessed, were in the past, sometimes a secret past: they were struck perhaps by the contrast between the solution of the play and the unresolved reality of what had happened to them.

But there was another reaction, equally important: an anger that bullying is allowed to go on. And with this a resolution to do something, to get in there before the long-term damage is done. The message of the final song ('Open the circle now . . . Don't keep bullying a secret . . .') has an added meaning for adults: Don't just wait for an incident to happen before you tackle bullying, do it now. In the audience that night were representatives of the funding bodies Neti-Neti relies on: every single one of them promised (and gave) more help.

And in each school Neti-Neti visits it is still the quality of response from the adults — the tutors, form teachers, PSE/Drama/English/Special Needs staff, and of course the Head – that I look for as a way of evaluating our work. If the drama takes root in them, a simple act of empathy can grow into something fruitful, lasting and worthwhile.

Footnote

'Only Playing, Miss': playscript/workshops, by Penny Casdagli and Francis Gobey, Trentham Books, 1990. The playscript and a full description of the workshops. ISBN: 0 948080 40 X. £9.95.

Only Playing, Miss: video (56 mins). The original stage play performed in English, Sign Language with some Bengali. £39.95.

Only Playing, Miss: playscript: with writings from young people. Neti-Neti, £2.50.

All available from Neti-Neti, 44 Gladsmuir Road, London N19 3JU. (Please add 75p P&P per book or video, 50p per script.)

CHAPTER 8

The Use of Theatre Workshop and Role Play in PSE in a Secondary School

Chris Housden

If a school is to confront the issue of bullying in an effective and meaningful way then there needs to be an understanding amongst the whole staff about the approach; its aims and objectives. There is a need for the coordination of ideas and for access to all pupils through the curriculum. This might be through Drama, PSE or tutorial time, but without this access then a school will not be able to meet its objectives. I will describe my own school's structure and approach in the hope that this will help you to consider critically those that prevail in your institution.

The school

The school is an 11–16 Comprehensive with approximately 800 pupils. It shares the teaching and administration of the Sixth Form Centre, which houses some 200 students. It is situated in a relatively affluent suburb of Nottingham where housing is almost entirely private and comparatively quite expensive. Seventy per cent of the pupils, however, are bussed into the school from the larger suburbs of Beeston and Chilwell. There is also a significant minority who come to the school from various other parts of Nottingham, out of the school's catchment area. The school is therefore comprised of a broad range of pupils of differing social and economic backgrounds and of differing academic abilities. Very few of our pupils experience material deprivation, but we have to deal with many problems resulting from emotional deprivation of differing complexities.

The school went comprehensive in September 1978, having previously been a selected Grammar School. Its evolution from Grammar to Comprehensive was a gradual process which was accelerated in 1982 by a change in Headteacher.

PSE in the school

The resulting change in ethos enabled me as the then newly appointed Head of Careers to begin the development of a Personal and Social Education programme. The detail of that development would provide material for a complete book. I will, therefore, simply outline the changes in structure, without explanation of how this was achieved.

PSE was initially introduced into the curriculum as a course for a particular group of 5th Year pupils. They were largely disaffected youngsters whom the highly academic grammar school system had failed and who were anxious to leave the school environment. For them the methodology employed in this course provided welcome relief from the very formal, academic lessons they were used to.

With the arrival of the new Headteacher came the opportunity for PSE to become a core subject, at least in years four and five. A team of teachers from many disciplines within the school came together voluntarily to teach PSE. Interest soon progressed to genuine enthusiasm as the subject began to have a positive impact on the school as a whole. Other staff, although not wishing to participate, supported what was being done; as a result PSE gradually increased its credibility in the eyes of both the staff and the pupils.

The present situation and, therefore, the vehicle used to develop the work on bullying, is that all pupils in the school from Year 1 to Year 5 have PSE on their timetable as a core subject.

The change in ethos was brought about by an adjustment of emphasis. Whilst still maintaining the academic traditions of the school, the pastoral organisation was given managerial support and status. Two new posts (that are particularly relevant here) were created; one was the post of Head of PSE ('D' Allowance) and the other Pastoral Co-ordinator (also 'D' Allowance). These two appointments have done much to ensure the status and influence of the pastoral part of school life, enabling a genuine mesh of the academic and pastoral support offered to pupils. In short, whilst we undoubtedly do not have a perfect school, we do have a caring environment in which the vast majority of pupils prosper.

It is difficult to say at this stage what the long term impact of the National Curriculum will be on the PSE structure. Discussions at senior management level would suggest that whilst there will be a need to reduce the time allocation (at least in the 4th and 5th Year, where PSE occupies 8 per cent of Curriculum time at the moment) there is a desire to retain some time for all pupils. This is, of course, a recognition of the important contribution that PSE makes in supporting pupils' personal development and thereby supporting the academic success that the school and the pupils are working towards. Our PSE syllabus is a product of more than one INSET event which were attended by PSE teachers along with representatives from the police, our school nurse, the Careers Service and governors.

Bullying – a problem?

A superficial look at the pupils working and relaxing together would not have suggested that a bullying problem exists at the school. There are few overt demonstrations of aggression; pupils are not obviously being physically abused by one another. It became clear to pastoral staff, however, that there was a problem of bullying of a more subtle nature. This was first brought out into the open in a public way at a meeting of the school Council.

The school Council was set up and is chaired by the Pastoral Co-ordinator in conjunction with one of the deputies. It is made up of a boy and a girl from each of the year groups 1–5 plus another member of staff and a school governor. Each of the pupils is democratically elected by their peers and reports back issues raised at the school Council to their year council.

Following a meeting of the school Council in early October 1989 my attention was drawn to this item which appeared in the minutes:

> BULLYING: All agreed that this was a persistent problem within the school and that solutions were hard to find. Certainly victims should tell someone, a teacher, the nurse, even an older pupil. It was felt that the matter should be brought out into the open in Form Periods and PSE lessons.

Reading that extract from the minutes determined me to respond in some way using the PSE structure of lessons as the vehicle for this.

I was motivated by three, for me, extremely important factors: firstly, that this request, though prompted by staff, had come from the pupils themselves; secondly, that in so doing they had recognised their PSE lessons as a suitable forum to bring the issue out in the open; and thirdly, the thought that we had pupils in the school who were suffering daily as a result of bullying. However subtle this might be it was unacceptable to me and I felt sure to the majority of my colleagues also.

Bullying is a topic that we had only touched on in some PSE lessons, with some pupils prior to the school Council meeting. It was obvious, therefore, we lacked material, ideas and experience at that stage.

Outside support

As I started to focus on relevant material we could use, bullying suddenly seemed to be the burning issue in the media and amongst other educationalists. My attention was drawn first to an article in the *Young Guardian*; a very moving story of a seventeen year old boy who took his own life after a prolonged period of bullying by former friends. At the end of the article mention was made of a London-based theatre company who were taking a play about bullying, called *Only Playing, Miss*, into London schools with great success (see Chapter 7).

I decided that I would write to the Neti-Neti Theatre Company, explain what I was trying to do and invite them to bring their play to Nottingham. At the same time I signalled my intention to colleagues by raising the issue of bullying at meetings I had with the 4th and 5th Year team and with the Tutor teams in Years 1, 2, and 3. These were not ad hoc meetings but part of a regular series of meetings designed to keep staff working together and feeling part of the process of development within the classroom.

Having done this I was made aware of some ideas that were already being tried in PSE lessons by one or two form tutors of the younger children; they too had responded to conversations which resulted from the school Council meeting and from staff pastoral meetings. Some of the work that was already being done with certain groups was imaginative and original. What was needed at this time was the co-ordination of ideas and the further gathering of information and resources so that this could be shared with all PSE staff.

I did not know at the time, but a series of events were about to unfold which would provide us with a unique opportunity to develop some exciting learning situations that would prove invaluable in the classroom.

I received a reply from the Neti-Neti Theatre Company quite

quickly, enclosing details of their play and indicating that they might be taking the company on a tour of schools outside of London in 1990/1991. I wrote back to them immediately, requesting that they include our school in their tour and confirming that we would meet the costs involved. The fee originally quoted was an amount I felt able to cover within my PSE budget allowance. Subsequently the amount was increased due to Arts Council funding cuts and it was necessary for me to approach the Headteacher to cover the deficit from other funds; this he readily agreed to do.

I was not intending to wait until the 1990/1991 academic year before tackling the issue in PSE. Since I see it as an on-going issue, not a one off, it seemed sensible to have something to focus on in the next academic year.

Around this time the BBC series 'Forty Minutes' produced a documentary on the subject of bullying. Several of the PSE team recorded this and we developed a lesson around it using extracts from the programme as a focus.

When we returned to school after Christmas I was contacted by one of the Neti-Neti producers, who had been approached by the Central Television company concerning their possible involvement in the making of a children's television programme about bullying. The theatre company, apart from performing plays in schools, had someone who also worked with pupils developing drama workshops. Central Television were anxious to film such a workshop in operation and Neti-Neti had spoken of the interest our school had shown in tackling the problem. I was asked if I would meet initially with one of the researchers from Central Television; this I readily agreed to do, in order to determine the aims of the programme.

I should make it clear that I am a firm believer in involving outside agencies wherever possible in school. We should not seek to make the education of pupils our sole preserve – there are many occasions when outside agencies working with teachers, as a team, can enrich the learning experiences of young people. This does, however, require a co-ordinated approach, where teachers and outside providers can plan together to ensure an effective learning experience. I would not, therefore, put someone in front of a group of youngsters without having determined beforehand the aims, objectives and methodology that were going to be employed.

Central Television's aims were admirable; they wanted to produce a twenty minute programme, for children, that might highlight the problem, whilst at the same time suggesting some strategies that victims and bullies might employ to escape from their unhappy situation. They wanted to show schools where some attempt was being made to confront the problem and the ways in which this was being done. What they offered us was very attractive; they would sponsor Neti-Neti to produce a drama workshop in our school, so that at an appropriate time, negotiated with both us and the Theatre Company, they might film some of the results.

Excited by the opportunity this offered us I immediately sought the help and guidance of one of our deputy heads who was herself part of the PSE team and a committed supporter of its ethos. Together with the researcher and producer from Central Television we explored the aims and objectives as presented to us, in order to reassure ourselves that the school, and in particular the pupils, would not be misrepresented in any way by the programme.

Having done this it was then necessary to seek approval from the Headteacher while he in turn needed approval from County Hall to allow the cameras in. Support from the Headteacher was immediate and after a concerted effort by himself, officers of the authority and Central Television, approval was given.

I kept interested parties in school (e.g. PSE teachers, tutors, English teachers) informed at all times what was happening, seeking their ideas and support as to how we might make best use of the opportunity afforded us. The English department were keen to be involved and offered a number of ideas as to how they might develop literacy and dramatic skills alongside the PSE programme and the Neti-Neti workshop.

I do not consider that involvement in the television programme was essential to the work that we did or are doing. It did raise the profile of the PSE and drama work that was done in school and it did pay for the workshop (Central TV sponsored Neti-Neti in this regard), but, as I hope will become clear, there are many activities in the classroom that can be effective in raising and opening up this issue without the need for television involvement.

Planning the drama workshop

The workshop was to take place immediately after the half term holiday of the Spring Term. In order to ensure that the detailed planning of both the Workshop and Central Television's involvement could be carried out, myself and the deputy head met the producer from Central Television again. I also arranged a day when Francis

Gobey, the education officer from the Neti-Neti Theatre Company, could come to school to meet myself, our Headmaster, the deputy Head, Head of English and the drama teacher who was to work alongside him in the workshops; we were also joined by the producer from Central Television.

A day was fixed, a timetable of informal meetings was organised, enabling arrangements to be made which suited all interested parties. These arrangements were made possible because of a willingness on everyone's part to co-operate so that we could all reap the maximum benefit from this opportunity. Meetings such as this are time consuming and difficult to set up, but for a project of this nature, or indeed any PSE project, it is essential to be working together as a team – school plus outside agencies together.

The workshops took place over three successive days – they were led by Francis Gobey and supported by our drama teacher. Our aim was to generate ideas amongst the workshop group that could be then transferred to PSE, English and Drama lessons. It was our intention to involve the workshop pupils in the development of learning experiences in the classroom. The group of 15 pupils involved was drawn from the 2nd and 3rd Years; they were of mixed ability, gender and race. There was a genuine attempt to reflect a true cross section of the school; all the pupils were volunteers. We chose 2nd and 3rd Years because we wanted to maximise the impact on year groups and it was our intention that our 1st Years would form the audience for the play *Only Playing, Miss*, although subsequently we decided to include our 2nd Years in the audience as well.

Although these were drama workshops, Francis did not rely solely on drama to examine the subject. Role play formed the basis for the work that was done, but he employed writing skills, poetry and oral communication as well.

The workshop group produced a questionnaire and then, using a tape recorder, interviewed, at random, fellow pupils during breaks and lunchtimes. Central Television filmed these interviews, along with some role play situations, before finally producing the programme 'Sticks and Stones' which was networked in March 1990. We were pleased with the way the programme dealt with the subject; it was both sensitive and enlightened.

Apart from the 'buzz' that having camera crews in school created, and involvement of the workshop group, we did gain quite a lot more from the process I have described. It was the first time that we had been involved as a staff in such an exercise and it stretched our organisation and co-ordination skills in a valuable way. The ideas and information that were gained from both Francis Gobey and the Central Television research provided us with a lot of material from which to create some challenging learning experiences for pupils.

Whilst we undoubtedly benefited from the Neti-Neti experience and from Francis Gobey's expertise, I don't think that it was crucial to the school's development of work on bullying. Drama workshops could be produced through a school's own drama department or, for schools without drama on the curriculum, through local theatre groups. It is certainly one way of highlighting the issue and in that sense would serve to support teachers who were trying to raise the awareness within school. There are, though, other ways in which concerned staff might approach this. These approaches are role play, the identification of positive and negative qualities and peer group surveys.

PSE lesson examples

I will illustrate role play by describing one particular learning experience in detail. I will describe it as though it was one lesson although in reality it could form the basis of several lessons depending on the time available. I would stress that these lessons have been constructed by practising teachers working as a team, pooling ideas and resources from various sources, having been stimulated by the Neti-Neti workshop and the Central Television programme, 'Sticks and Stones'; they have not been taken from a textbook.

The first approach requires few, if any, resources and relies almost entirely on role play and oral feedback. It can be achieved in a normal classroom and with a normal sized group – we did it with groups of approximately twenty-five. I will set this out in the form of a lesson plan: explanations are within brackets:

LESSON PLAN – BULLYING

Aims/objectives: To explore through role play, the subject of bullying from the pupils' perspective. To help pupils to determine what they consider bullying to be, the effects it has on individuals and the community and to establish some strategies to help alleviate the problem in our school.

(1) **Outline the aims and objectives to the class.**
(2) **Ask them to form themselves into single sex groups.** (You could stipulate the number in the group, but natural variations in size of

groups served to create greater variety in the role plays. We decided on single sex groups because in our experience the vast majority of bullying occurs male on male and female on female and rarely between the sexes).

(3) **Tell the groups that their task is to plan and perform a short role play** which for them typifies the bullying that is to be found within our institution. Stress that all members of the group must have a role to play, even if that role is only the passive one of an onlooker.

(4) **Allocate a space where each group can plan and practise.** (If possible it is desirable at this time to use another room nearby, in order to split the class or, if this is impossible, use some space in a corridor. I appreciate with some pupils this may be problematic and that it will obviously depend on the group and your relationship with them as to whether you feel able to do this).

(5) **Move between the groups** noting how they are organising themselves as well as the type of scenarios they are creating. Do not interfere with the groups unless invited by them to do so; do not try to inflict your views on them; this should be owned entirely by them.

(6) **Give them sufficient time to determine and practise their roles.** (On average we found this took between 20 and 25 minutes, though this will obviously vary according to the group).

(7) When you consider the groups are ready, bring them back to the classroom where **they should, each group in turn, perform their role plays.** (The formality of the classroom needs to be broken down at this stage, putting desks or tables to one side, creating a space in which to perform the role plays and sitting the 'audience' informally).

(8) When all the groups have performed their role plays **encourage discussion about the scenarios** by asking them to consider the following questions:

- WERE THEY 'REAL' SITUATIONS?
- WERE THEY ALL BULLYING?
- WHICH OF THEM BEST REPRESENTED THE REALITY IN OUR SCHOOL?

(Depending on the group these questions could be discussed by the whole group together, or in small groups of three or four and then fed back to the whole group. Discussion about the role plays, in our experience, can be lengthy and animated, producing a myriad of opinions about the types of bullying that occur and their relative seriousness).

(9) When you feel that useful discussion has ended **ask the group to choose one of the role plays that they most identify with,** for use in the next part of the lesson.

(10) **Introduce the idea of the 'Bully Court' to the group.** Check through

discussion that they are all familiar with what a 'Bully Court' is. (The idea of the 'Bully Court' was promoted by KIDSCAPE to find practical ways of keeping children safe from a variety of dangers including bullying. Our pupils were already familiar with the idea as a result of having seen the 'Sticks and Stones' video (Central Television) which highlights this particular approach to dealing with the problem. It was not our intention to necessarily encourage the idea, but to use it as a learning experience in a role play situation. See also Chapter 3).

(11) **The whole group should now decide:**
  (a) How should such a court be organised?
  (b) How many people should be on the panel?
  (c) Who should they be?
  (d) What questions should be asked?
  (e) What should be the role of the teacher?
  (f) What punishments should the court administer, if any?

(12) When this has been decided, volunteers from those not involved in roles in the chosen bullying scenario should form the panel in the court. Those not directly involved in the role play should act as observers, noting down problems, concerns and the strengths and weaknesses of what is taking place.

(13) **The teacher at this point should let the pupils take control of what happens next** and should assume the role given to them by the group. (This may appear unwise to some of you, but our experience is that, by this stage, even the more demanding groups were so involved in what was happening that the role of the teacher could safely be determined by the group).

(14) **The role play should now be enacted** with everyone directly involved being interviewed by the 'Court'; bully, victim and witnesses. Allow proceedings to be determined by the pupils for as long as is deemed practicable.

(15) When proceedings have reached a natural conclusion, or indeed when time dictates, the teacher should now take back control and initiate a discussion about what has happened. Ask the pupils, still in role, **how they feel about what has taken place.** Ask the victim, the bully or bullies, the witnesses and finally the panel who made up the 'Court'. Ask the observers for their views. Encourage listening skills and reasoned argument, to create an atmosphere in which feelings can be expressed openly.

An interesting situation occurred when I was doing this with a group of fourth years (15 year olds). When the panel interviewed the bully she denied categorically everything she was accused of. Despite persistent questioning she stuck to her story. One of the two witnesses corroborated the victim's story, but the other witness forgot a vital piece of information and actually was incorrect in her description of another aspect of the story. The error was a genuine one on the part of the girl who was playing this role. The panel were thrown into confusion by this and after much debate had to conclude that they were unable to decide on the truth of what happened because of the numerous inconsistencies. This was a worthwhile learning experience shared by the whole group and opened up an animated discussion of what strategies were likely to be effective when attempting to confront bullying.

(16) Split the class into working groups giving them the task of deciding what advice could be given to the following people to help them assist in doing something about bullying:

    (a) Adults – parents and teachers

    (b) Victims

    (c) Bullies

    (d) Others (the people who stand by and watch)

(This could be divided up so that each group prepared an advice sheet for one of the groups of people listed. We found that this was quite an effective way of dividing up the task, whilst not negating anyone else from having an input, as the rest of the group were able to comment during the feedback session. KIDSCAPE have produced a series of advice sheets about bullying aimed at VICTIMS, BULLIES, PARENTS, TEACHERS and others. Central Television also produced a pack for schools as a result of their research for 'Sticks and Stones'. This information was used by us when assessing with the pupils the strengths and weaknesses that came from their endeavours).

(17) **Feedback from each group**, encouraging constructive criticism by the whole group. Collate ideas to be reviewed at a later date. Lesson ends.

The length of time the process I have just described might take is between two and four hours. It will depend on the nature of the group whether they feel at ease with the role play and how much time is available in a session. There are a number of identifiable stages, however, which might form a natural break between sessions.

It took me four hours with one group of 25 (15 year olds) to reach stage 17; I had them for two × two hour sessions. If you do not have access to that amount of time in one go (and I appreciate many schools don't), then it is likely that greater overall time would be needed, as it would be necessary to back-track and reinforce at the start of each session.

Other approaches

What I have described here represents but one of a number of different approaches which have been developed by the PSE team at the school. Another approach which was used to introduce the idea of bullying was to identify, with the pupils, positive and negative qualities to be found in individuals. We took time to help individuals to recognise the positive qualities in themselves and in others, before introducing the idea of negative qualities. Having identified these negative qualities we provided the pupils with an exercise to determine which of these qualities had the most effect on other people. We then put it into the context of school by suggesting ways in which this might manifest itself in school, e.g. disruption of lessons, truancy, rudeness, theft, work not done, bullying and so on. We then asked the pupils to decide which of these things were most serious and why. This then enabled us to focus more closely on bullying and move more easily into the lesson I previously described in detail.

Another approach, which was used with the younger pupils, was to get them to research the problems amongst their peers. They prepared questions and surveyed other classes before producing statistics in the form of graphs. This was done by a group of first years before the Neti-Neti Workshop took place in school, but perhaps not surprisingly, the questions the pupils from the first year group wanted to ask were almost identical to those prepared by the pupils in the Neti-Neti Workshop.

We have also used both the 'Forty Minutes' documentary (BBC) and 'Sticks and Stones' (Central TV) as the focus for lessons; not as lessons in themselves but as a support for meaningful discussion.

There are other ways of raising the awareness through poetry, essay writing, drama and art work (see also Chapter 6). As I write this we are only two months away from a performance of the Penny Casdagli play *Only Playing, Miss* which will be performed by the Neti-Neti Theatre Company in front of our 1st and 2nd Years.

Having rested the subject for a short while we are set to introduce it again to prepare the pupils for the coming performance so that we may get as much as possible from it. Our English, Drama and Art departments, along with form tutors through PSE, are planning once again to raise the awareness level in the school as a whole and encourage pupils to talk openly about the problem, along with all staff, so that together we may seek to make our school free of the unhappiness that bullying brings.

As I said at the beginning, it needs to be a whole school approach and this must be co-ordinated if it is to be effective. There may be need for INSET; there is certainly a need for dialogue amongst the staff and

CHAPTER 9

The North East Derbyshire Bullying Project:
A Multi-Disciplinary Support Network

Martin Wilkinson and Simon Priest

Background

Despite the rather wordy title what follows is intended to be a down-to-earth account of a group of professionals from a wide variety of backgrounds getting together to share their concerns, support each other and identify good practice with regard to reducing bullying and aggressive behaviour.

North East Derbyshire is a mixture of small industrial or mining towns and villages located in a rural setting adjoining the Peak District. The school-age population is around 42,000 but more importantly they attend over 160 local schools of all descriptions. This part of the world fares well on most social and educational indices although the area is by no means affluent and the bias is most certainly towards the industrial manufacturing industries.

In the early days of this project, amidst inconclusive discussions about the size and nature of the problem in this area, the authors noted with interest research conducted in some Sheffield secondary schools by Yates and Smith (1989). Although this large industrial conurbation is barely half an hour's drive away from the centre of North East Derbyshire there are significant demographic and cultural differences, many of which are the source of considerable local pride and self-identity. The international research on the frequency and nature of bullying behaviour with regard to geographical and social factors seemed insufficient to justify us extrapolating from the Sheffield findings. With regret, the authors finally accepted that it was not possible to gauge fully the size of such a complex and widespread phenomenon as bullying but that this lack of knowledge should not be used as an excuse for inactivity on the part of those adults charged with the well-being of children.

The project

Martin Wilkinson is a member of a Behavioural Support Team who work with teachers and children in local schools with the aim of enhancing a school's ability to retain and a child's ability to remain in mainstream education. Simon Priest is an Educational Psychologist who has been running workshops with teachers on bullying since 1987. During 1989 the authors found themselves increasingly into discussions about bullying and noted a number of workers in other agencies who were also concerned about the problem. The decision seemed to be either to continue with these varied and individual approaches or to attempt some form of multi-disciplinary coordination. Given the enormous media attention to bullying throughout 1989 (which extended to bullying in the Army, prisons, Youth Training Schemes, workplace and even in the staffroom) the time seemed right to capitalise on this interest and attempt a higher profile approach which might potentially involve large numbers of schools in the area. Consequently, interested members of the Behavioural Support Team and Psychological Service were invited to an initial Steering Group meeting along with colleagues from the Education Welfare Service and Child and Family Therapy Team. The respective approaches to working with children involved in bullying are illustrated in Figure 9.1. This Steering Group, numbering between 6 and 12 individuals, first met in December 1989 and since then have met approximately monthly up until the time of writing (November 1990). The authors took on the task of project coordinators (including, amongst other things, spending long shifts in front of an over-heated photocopier!).

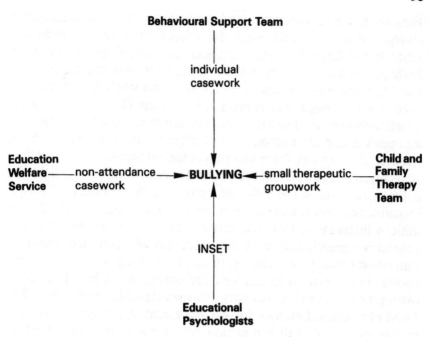

Figure 9.1 The main interests and background of the Steering Group

Aims

At this first Steering Group meeting four aims were identified which appear to have survived the test of time relatively well:

(1) To raise awareness of bullying in schools and other settings.
(2) To collect and disseminate information and ideas.
(3) To establish multi-disciplinary links.
(4) To support and develop anti-bullying projects.

During this early stage the Steering Group were slightly apprehensive about the possibility of generating unjustified concern in the community or adverse publicity by launching a project concerned with bullying. They felt it important to stress publicly that there was no evidence whatsoever that bullying was increasing in the area and, in fact, there was a subjective perception that over the years the problem had decreased. Nevertheless, the workers involved felt that bullying and hostility were still a significant part of many children's lives and that there was no room for complacency. Apart from the fortuitous media attention, the Steering Group noted vigorous LEA initiatives on Equal Opportunities, Education for All, Personal and Social

Education, Child Protection and Violence in the Workplace which clearly complement this particular theme. Four recommendations made in the Elton Report ('Discipline in Schools' 1989) considered bullying concurrently with racialism. More internationally, the United Nations were in the process of ratifying a Children's Bill of Rights.

In order to begin the process the Steering Group wrote to the Headteachers of all the schools inviting anyone who was interested to an open meeting after school, to be held in the building shared by the Behavioural Support Team and Psychological Service: these meetings were advertised as Bullying Forums and a series of three were held. On a practical note, the logistics of writing to this number of people required the support and understanding of line-managers as well as an initial willingness to fund the cost out of local service budgets. The process was greatly helped by the regular delivery service by the Area Education Office to all schools. In addition to teachers, the Steering Group wrote to local Social Services Offices and Child Protection Managers as well as the Advisory Teachers (Special Education), PSE, Child Protection, Learning for All and Equal Opportunities. Having realised in retrospect their omission, Youth and Community Workers were invited to subsequent forums but, at the time of writing, no satisfactory links have yet been established with Colleges of Further Education.

The Bullying Forums

The first Bullying Forum was held in February 1990 and attended by 63 participants representing over 20 schools along with education and health support services as well as Dr Peter Smith and colleagues from Sheffield University who introduced the topic by overviewing the national dimensions. For the main part of this first session participants discussed the following issues in small groups:

(a) What are our concerns with regard to bullying?
(b) What do we currently do about the problem?
(c) What might we do in the future?

The coordinators did think ahead to having nominated group leaders to facilitate discussions as well as note-takers who recorded the conversations in a standardised format to enable a proper collation of everybody's viewpoint. As the Steering Group had hoped, these early talks produced a wealth of ideas based not on introspection or psychological theory but on many years experience with young people. These

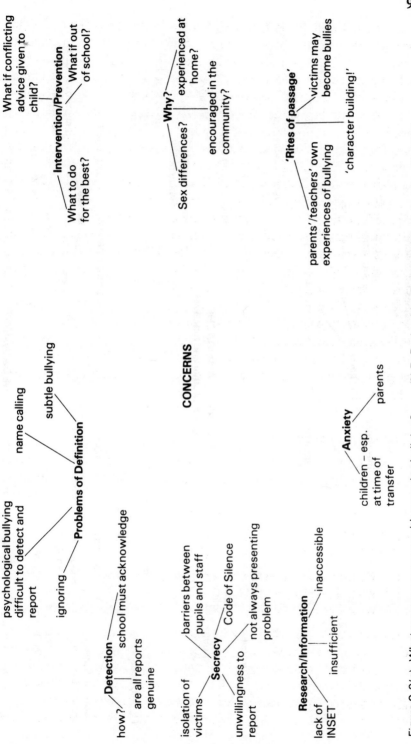

Figure 9.2(a) What are our concerns with regard to bullying?   (N.E. Derbyshire Bullying Forum No 1. – 8.2.90)

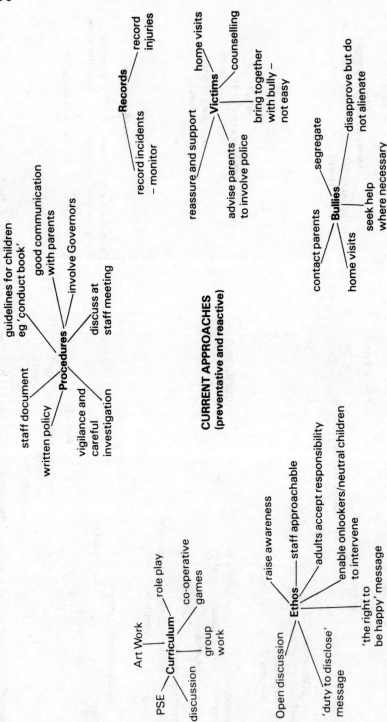

Records
record incidents – monitor
record injuries

Victims
reassure and support
advise parents to involve police
bring together with bully – not easy
home visits
counselling

Bullies
contact parents
home visits
segregate
seek help where necessary
disapprove but do not alienate

Procedures
staff document
written policy
guidelines for children eg 'conduct book'
good communication with parents
involve Governors
discuss at staff meeting
vigilance and careful investigation

CURRENT APPROACHES
(preventative and reactive)

Curriculum
Art Work
PSE
discussion
role play
co-operative games
group work

Ethos
Open discussion
'duty to disclose' message
raise awareness
staff approachable
adults accept responsibility
enable onlookers/neutral children to intervene
'the right to be happy' message

Figure 9.2(b)   What do we currently do about the problem?   (NE Derbyshire Bullying Forum No 1 – 8.2.90)

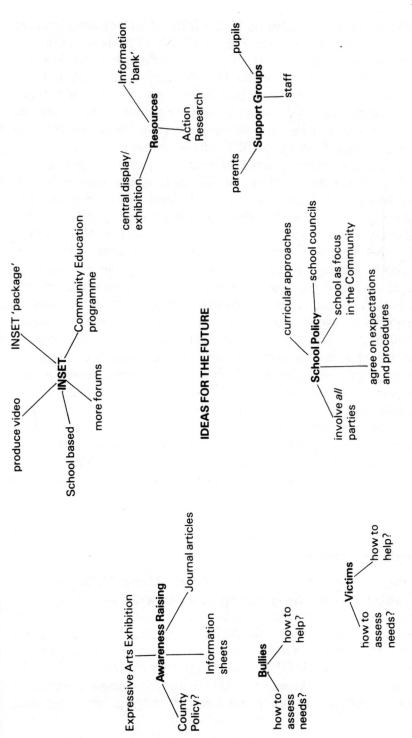

IDEAS FOR THE FUTURE

INSET
- produce video
- INSET 'package'
- School based
- Community Education programme
- more forums

Resources
- central display/exhibition
- Information 'bank'
- Action Research

Support Groups
- parents
- pupils
- staff

School Policy
- curricular approaches
- school councils
- school as focus in the Community
- involve *all* parties
- agree on expectations and procedures

Awareness Raising
- Expressive Arts Exhibition
- Journal articles
- County Policy?
- Information sheets

Bullies
- how to assess needs?
- how to help?

Victims
- how to assess needs?
- how to help?

Figure 9.2 (c) What might we do in the future?   (NE Derbyshire Bullying Forum No 1 – 8.2.90)

deliberations were written up in the form of leaflets and circulated back to the participants (see Figures 9.2a, b, c) along with other information which the authors felt might be helpful to practitioners.

It had been decided at the outset that the project leaflets should have a recognisable 'house style' with colour coding for each leaflet/topic. Although no graphic design facilities were readily available and the choice of a suitable logo proved elusive, a compromise was achieved by one of the authors on his BBC micro-processor.

It came as no surprise to the Steering Group that the agenda set at the first forum reflected interest in bullying behaviour both at the level of individual children and also at the level of whole-school and community approaches. Bullying Forum No 2 was held in March 1990 and dealt with the latter considerations whilst Forum No 3, held in May 1990 dealt with some contemporary approaches to individual casework looking at national and local approaches. There is insufficient scope to deal with the content of these meetings other than to note an unanimous perception that bullying is a complex phenomenon involving the whole community: the conceptualisation of bullying as being a problem unique to relatively small numbers of 'deviant' children was firmly rejected. As a consequence, talk about whole-school approaches invariably involved parents, governors and the wider community as well as the formal and 'hidden' curricula. At the level of individual youngsters, attention soon shifted away from those children more immediately involved towards consideration of the role of the onlooker. It was especially illuminating for some participants to borrow the psychological model of 'bystander reaction theory' to look at the issues of support or disapproval for the bullying and whether this is actively or passively expressed by the peer group (see Figure 9.3).

Present developments

By the completion of Form No 3 the Steering Group felt that there was no further place for this type of open meeting and that the project was now moving into its second phase. At this last forum, in accompanying letters to school and during the course of their day-to-day work, the Steering Group offered their support to any teacher colleagues who felt that they would like to initiate any work around the theme of bullying. We were not able to identify changes in perceived levels of bullying, let alone real levels of bullying, but it did seem

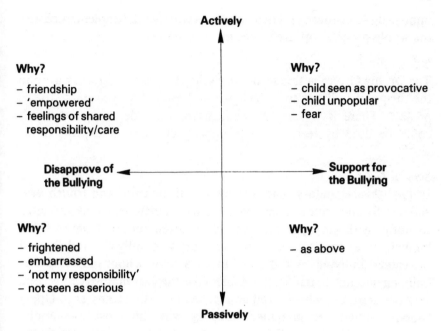

Figure 9.3 Bullying: the role of Onlookers

reasonable to hope that the project would act as stimulus for some new work in schools.

The meetings have been characterised by exceptional levels of commitment and interest whilst the resulting leaflets have been well received. The crucial question though for most of those involved was whether schools felt the need or capability to launch proactive initiatives in the face of innumerable competing demands on their time.

By necessity, this chapter is a 'snapshot view' of a project under way. As the academic year 1990/91 started the following pieces of work were ready to take off:

School No 1
Two teachers in this local secondary school are surveying the views of fourth year pupils on bullying in order to produce practical advice for youngsters and their parents.

School No 2
The headteacher of this primary school is concerned about aggressive behaviour out of the classroom at break- and lunch-times which includes bullying. There are plans to video some of this behaviour and then present it back to the children, inviting them to suggest ways of

improving the situation. Their solutions will then be implemented and the whole process captured once more on video.

School No 3
The Drama Group at this secondary school are planning work around the theme of bullying to be videoed and offered as a resource to the project. There is widespread enthusiasm for video material which could be used by teachers to prompt discussions or expressive art work.

School No 4
In 1987 this secondary school surveyed all the third and fourth year children by anonymous questionnaires which included items unrelated to bullying. Eighty per cent of the children reported never being bullied, up to four per cent reported frequent bullying, and the rest occasional bullying. A different survey at that school indicated that bullying was not a significant problem for the vast majority of second year children, but when asked about the impending transfer to Upper School, anticipated/imagined bullying was the most commonly-reported anxiety. When the same group of children were questioned again in their third year at the Upper School they reported that the reality was very different and for the vast majority bullying was not a problem. More recently, a team of staff at this school (who are members of the Derbyshire Secondary Development Project and hence receive an extra staffing increment for Project purposes) are considering how to link up with their feeder schools to launch a wide, community-based initiative. Two of the headteachers from their feeder school attended the bullying forums where they expressed very similar concerns about the macho male-stereotype in the community which particularly affects styles of parenting and approaches to solving inter-personal disputes.

Elsewhere in Derbyshire but outside of the North East, links have been made with four secondary schools largely as a result of publicity surrounding the project. One of these is completing an information gathering survey whilst another places its emphasis on drama and assemblies. The two other schools have each launched a range of initiatives intended to involve large numbers of staff and pupils. In one of these the bias is very firmly towards involving youngsters as active participants and there are also plans to link up with a national theatre company. The fourth school is coordinating its work by means of a powerful working party involving parent and community representatives as well as members of local agencies and services.

Future plans

Given the continuing support of line managers, senior officers and elected members, a number of developments are envisaged and currently being actively pursued. To encourage those schools who have embarked upon work and to share their experiences with others, a one-day conference is being planned for February 1991 with a very firm emphasis on the local community and practicality. Up until now teachers have participated in their own time but there was a clear feeling on this occasion that supply cover should be offered if at all possible. Such a bid is about to be considered by a locally-managed fund whose purpose is to support staff development activities in community education involving staff from different sections or educational phases.

Along with the conference it is hoped to mount an exhibition of children's art work around the theme of bullying and both of these events will be announced to schools in the near future via a news sheet which may also give details of the sort of work discussed above.

Lastly, one of the authors is drawing together and amplifying the leaflets into substantial resource documents. In particular, there is a desire to offer interested schools a possible framework for drawing up a whole school policy to combat bullying which seems likely to be very similar to guidelines circulated by the LEA last year with regard to combatting racial harassment in schools.

Conclusions

What has been achieved so far? At the very least professionals from different settings have met together to discuss common concerns and share good practice. Many teachers and members of the LEA support services have enthused about this style of collaborative working compared with the more usual crisis-management. Apart from the obvious benefits of sharing ideas and working with colleagues in novel ways there has been a process of empowerment whereby individuals or small groups of individuals have returned to their institution armed with information and a mandate for change. In schools in particular, personified by the Derbyshire Secondary Development Project, there is a move away from the old hierarchical management structure to a flatter, more egalitarian, 'middle-out' process whereby teachers can

102

take a more active part in the running of their schools. The principal roles of this project now are to act as a resource centre or information 'clearing house' and to offer support during change, in many ways a microcosm of the role of all LEA support services in the nineties.

CHAPTER 10

A Survey Service for Schools on Bully/Victim Problems

Yvette Ahmad, Irene Whitney and Peter K. Smith

The level of bullying and victimisation in schools is now being recognised as a problem which needs to be addressed. The survey service is designed for junior, middle and secondary schools interested and concerned about this issue. It provides a package of information about the extent of the problem in their school in particular, about where the problems are located (such as specific areas within the school, or classes where a high level of bullying occurs), and other information which could be of use in planning a school response to the issue.

The origins of the survey service

The questionnaire used is a modification of one devised by Dan Olweus at the University of Bergen in Norway (copyright for use of the questionnaire is currently with Dan Olweus). With the help of a grant from the ESRC, Swindon, we piloted out the questionnaire in Britain, and modified it slightly. Although an English-language version of the questionnaire had been provided by Professor Olweus, the wording was changed slightly to conform with current English usage. We also verified that an anonymous questionnaire of this type was a reliable way of finding out about the extent of bully/victim problems in schools (Ahmad and Smith, 1990). At this time, a few schools participated in an investigation of the level of bullying in the South Yorkshire region (the results of which are discussed in Chapter 1). This involved a full-time researcher who administered the questionnaires in the schools. Subsequent to this, more schools became interested in finding out about the level of bullying in their school, and it became clear that one researcher could not cope with the volume of interest.

With a grant from the Calouste Gulbenkian Foundation, we then developed a package 'survey service for schools', with detailed instructions on how to administer the questionnaires being provided to the schools themselves. A somewhat similar scheme had already been tried in Norway. The survey service was itself piloted on several middle and secondary schools, and feedback obtained from the schools, before the service reached its present form. All the schools were generally satisfied with the layout of instructions and found the portfolio extremely useful. However, slight modifications were made.

The current version of the survey service

There are two versions of the questionnaire – one for junior/middle schools, suitable for children aged 8 to 11 years; and one for secondary schools, suitable for children aged over 11. They are very similar, differing mainly in the number of response options to some questions, the use of *children* in the junior version and *young person* in the senior version, and details of the administration. In addition, following feedback from the middle schools in our pilot project, we provided a version of the questionnaire for junior/middle schools with a bigger print face for children with reading or learning difficulties.

The current version of the survey service package includes the following:

○ A quota of questionnaires appropriate for the school (with some of the larger print version if necessary).
○ Information to the Headteacher on selection of administrators and where to return the questionnaires after completion.
○ Clear instructions for the administrators to maintain standardised procedures.
○ A school information questionnaire for the Headteacher to fill out and return, requiring information about size, location and population of school (this is used for research purposes to examine whether these factors affect the level of bullying in schools).
○ A copy of *Bullying: A Positive Response*, by D. Tattum and G. Herbert (March 1990).

○ A Childline poster which can be put up by the school, with a telephone number for children to use if they wish.

Administration of the survey

The administration of the questionnaire was carefully thought out in relation to sustaining anonymity for the pupils; and systematic procedures are outlined so that each school's results should be comparable. The Headteacher is requested to assign administrators to classes which they do not usually teach. (In our pilot work, the three secondary schools found it difficult to swap around teachers to administer the questionnaire due to the size of the schools. Two schools opted for the use of form periods to give out the questionnaires (form tutors were the administrators). The third school brought all the pupils together at assembly and seated separately; extra administrators were used to monitor the pupils).

There are detailed step-by-step instructions for the administrators to follow. The preliminary instructions include the following points: to seat pupils separately; to explain to pupils the purpose of the questionnaire; to explain that the questionnaire remains anonymous. The administrator reads out the instructions and then reads out the definition of bullying. This definition, which follows closely that used by Professor Olweus in Norway, is given in figure 10.1.

For junior/middle school pupils the administrator then normally reads each question through with the class. They are also told if they have any difficulties to raise their hand. For secondary school pupils, the administrator usually lets the pupils proceed at their own speed after reading through the first page with them. The administrator

---

We say a child is BEING BULLIED, or picked on, when another child, or a group of children, say nasty or unpleasant things to him or her. It is also bullying when a child is hit, kicked, threatened, locked inside a room, sent nasty notes, when no one ever talks to them and things like that. These things can happen frequently and it is difficult for the child being bullied to defend himself or herself. It is also bullying when a child is teased repeatedly in a nasty way.
But it is NOT BULLYING when two children of about the same strength have the odd fight or quarrel.

N.B. This differs slightly from the version of Professor Olweus, by including 'sent nasty notes' and 'when no one ever talks to them' as additional examples of bullying, which we have found to be more frequent in girls than boys.

Figure 10.1 The definition of bullying used in the survey service

9. Have you been bullied by one, or several, children?	A	I haven't been bullied at school this term
	B	mainly by one boy
	C	by several boys
	D	mainly by one girl
	E	by several girls
	F	by both boys and girls

13. What do you do when you see a child of your age being bullied at school?	A	nothing, it's none of my business
	B	nothing, but I think I ought to try and help
	C	I try and help him or her in some way

19. How often have you taken part in bullying other children at school this term?	A	I haven't bullied anyone at school this term
	B	once or twice
	C	sometimes
	D	about once a week
	E	several times a week

Figure 10.2 Examples of three questions from the survey questionnaire

makes a note of any pupils with learning or reading difficulties and any problems that arise when administering the questionnaire. The questionnaires are then collected, placed in an envelope which is sealed and returned to the Headteacher.

The questionnaire consists of around 19 (junior/middle) or 20 (secondary) questions, sometimes expanded to 26 questions for research purposes. A range of different aspects of bullying are covered such as:

- How often are you bullied at school?
- In what way have you been bullied?
- Where did you get bullied?
- Have you been bullied by one, or several, children?
- How often have you taken part in bullying other children at school?
- Has the teacher talked to you about your bullying other children at school?

Examples of the layout of the questionnaire are shown in figure 10.2, which illustrates questions 9, 13 and 19 of the research version of the questionnaire.

Production of the portfolio

Once the main questionnaires are completed, they are returned to us

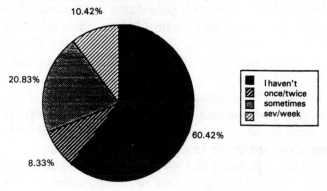

HOW OFTEN ARE YOU BULLIED AT SCHOOL? boys

10.42%

20.83%

8.33%

60.42%

I haven't
once/twice
sometimes
sev/week

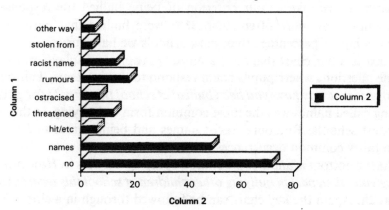

IN WHAT WAY HAVE YOU BEEN BULLIED? girls

Column 1

other way
stolen from
racist name
rumours
ostracised
threatened
hit/etc
names
no

0   20   40   60   80

Column 2

Column 2

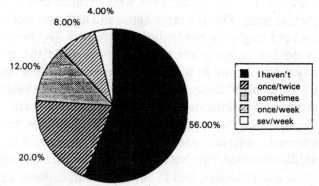

HAVE YOU BULLIED AT SCHOOL? class 2h

4.00%

8.00%

12.00%

20.0%

56.00%

I haven't
once/twice
sometimes
once/week
sev/week

Figure 10.3 Sample charts from the survey service portfolio

for analysis. After some weeks a portfolio of results is returned to the school for their use. This provides a detailed set of results with an analysis of each question in turn for the whole school. The results are also broken down into sex differences and class differences for specific items on the questionnaire. Many of the results are shown in pie chart form, and some as bar charts, to make points of interest readily accessible to the teachers. A sample of three such charts are shown in figure 10.3, from different schools; in all cases, though, the answers are referring to the previous term at the school, the questionnaire having been given about five to eight weeks into the term.

At the top in figure 10.3 is a pie diagram for a sample school showing the results for *How often have you been bullied at school this term?* : for boys. The key chart on the right hand side can be followed through on the pie chart in a clockwise manner. Over this period about 8% of boys were bullied once or twice, 21% sometimes and 10% several times a week. If we take as our criterion of being bullied the responses 'sometimes' or more often, then 31% were bullied that particular term; a higher percentage than most schools we have surveyed.

Next is a bar chart diagram; a more appropriate display form for some questions where pupils could respond to several items. This one is for *In what way have you been bullied at school this term?* : for girls. Being called names was the most common form of bullying, in this as in most schools. Rumours, racist names and being threatened were also fairly common occurrences.

At the bottom is another pie chart displaying answers to *How often have you taken part in bullying other children at school this term?* : for class 2h. Again the key chart can be followed through in a clockwise manner. In Class 2h, 20% have bullied once or twice, 12% sometimes, 8% once a week, and 4% several times a week. Taken from the criteria 'sometimes' or more often, 24% were engaged in bullying others that particular term. This is a large figure and indicates a class about which the school might be particularly concerned. (Although the children who do the bullying are not identified, since the questionnaire is anonymous, it may in practice be fairly easy for a teacher or other adult to identify these children, if not known already, by discreet questioning and interviewing of children in the class).

The top and bottom figures differ slightly in that the bottom figure has an extra criterion 'once a week'. The top figure is an example from a middle school and the bottom figure from a secondary school. In the original questionnaire, and in our first modifications, we assumed that secondary school pupils would be able to cope adequately with more mmultiple choice items. Our most recent modification does however equate the questionnaires with five response choices for this question (separating 'about once a week' and 'several times a week').

The portfolio provides results for the school as a whole for all items on the questionnaire (except for one to be explained shortly). There is also a breakdown for particular questions of sex differences and class differences. Sex differences are reported for the following questions:

> *How often have you been bullied at school this term?*
> *In what way have you been bullied?*
> *Have you been bullied by one, or several, children?*
> *What do you do when you see a child of your age being bullied at school?*
> *How often have you taken part in bullying other children at school this term?*
> *Where did you get bullied this term?*
> *What do you think about children who bully others?*

Results for each class are reported for the following questions:

> *How often have you been bullied at school this term?*
> *How often have you taken part in bullying other children at school this term?*

The answers to one question were not included in the portfolio. This question requested information about whether the pupil was being bullied by anyone else at school or outside of school. It was an open-ended question which pupils could answer if they wished. The results so far are being used for research purposes to gauge the extent of other kinds of bullying, which the main questionnaire items on peer bullying in school would not be picking up.

The portfolio also includes written information about the results, and an indication of how the school's results compare to other schools generally. It concludes with a summary sheet of the results, and an information sheet giving some ideas on how to tackle the problem of bullying and further references to resources and books on the topic.

In our pilot work, we have found that schools do feel the portfolio provides a useful service to them. As the questionnaire itself shows, many pupils who are bullied may not have talked to teachers or parents about it. Teachers may often feel that there is some problem of bullying in their school, without being too certain of its nature or extent. The survey will reveal whether these worries are justified, and will locate the nature and extent of the problem so that interventions can be targetted to most effect.

Use of the survey for research purposes

The primary use of the survey is for the benefit of schools. However it is also useful for research purposes, in two ways. First, it can start to build up a national picture of school variations, and suggest reasons for these. Second, it can be used to assess the effects of interventions. Both of these kinds of use are currently underway.

School variations

For this purpose, we make use of the school information questionnaire mentioned earlier. This asks for information such as:

- Number of pupils in the school to nearest hundred:
- Average class size:
- Is the school in a primarily urban or rural setting?
- A breakdown in approximate percentage terms of racial mix of the school:

White;	Pakistani;	Somali;
Afro-Caribbean;	Bangladeshi;	Chinese;
Indian;	Yemeni;	Other.

In the pilot work for the survey, five schools participated, three from the South Yorkshire region (two middle and one secondary school); one from the West Yorkshire region (secondary school level) and one from a London Borough (secondary school level). All five schools were different in racial mix, location and size, so as to provide a variety of experience with the questionnaire. Four of the schools were located in the inner city and one in a rural setting. Schools varied in size from 100 to 1100 pupils. Racial mix varied from two schools being approximately 100% white to the other three schools varying from 10% to 54% of other ethnic origin.

We found that the survey service was an effective and efficient way of collecting information about the level of bullying in schools. The pupils' responses were consistent, with only a 3 to 4% error factor across comparable questions. The results from the schools were clear that levels of bullying do vary considerably from school to school (as well as from class to class within a school). Owing to only five schools participating in the pilot survey, we cannot yet determine what factors affect the level of bullying in schools, but this information will contribute to a body of information which is accumulating. In the near future, data will be obtained for 24 schools in the Sheffield LEA (see below); and a broader picture will emerge as the survey is offered on a more national basis.

Evaluating the success of interventions

The survey can be used in a particular school to assess levels of bully/victim problems before, and after, some planned intervention has taken place. An example of this with one middle school which introduced group work, and a bully court, in certain years, is discussed in Chapter 3. The survey will identify the levels of bullying experienced within each class, and year, so (as in this example) it may be possible to compare changes in those classes which did experience the intervention, with those which did not. Alternatively, if the intervention is at the whole school level, the survey will show whether absolute levels have declined. Since absolute levels of bullying might also vary with such factors as time of year, or even specific historical events (for example, the Rushdie affair in 1989, and diverse reactions to it, might have temporarily increased incidents of racial harassment), it may be more convincing if results at that school can be compared with a similar school which did not experience the intervention.

The survey is currently being used in this way to evaluate the effects of interventions in twenty schools in one (Sheffield) LEA. These will include junior/middle and secondary schools in all areas of the city, with a wide range of school sizes, locations, catchment areas and school policies. Each school will be receiving a survey service report, or portfolio, around March 1991. This work is being funded by the Calouste Gulbenkian Foundation. Following this, with support from the DES, an advice team will discuss an intervention package appropriate for each school. The implementation of the agreed package will be monitored. Two years after the first survey, a second survey will be given to examine what changes in levels and kind of bullying have taken place, in each of these schools.

Participating schools will be given feedback directly on the results of their own interventions. However, the effectiveness of the interventions generally will be considered in the light of the overall pattern of results from the surveys, as well as the knowledge gained during the monitoring process. This information will be made available subsequently in a form readily accessible to all schools.

Interested in the survey service?

If your school is interested in the survey service then it may be possible to provide it, at a costed fee. Please contact:

Dr. P. K. Smith, Department of Psychology, PO Box 603, Western Bank, Sheffield S10 2UR.

CHAPTER 11

Developing a Co-ordinated Approach on Bullying/Victim Problems

Nottinghamshire Education Committee

The background

In October 1989 the Nottinghamshire Advisory and Inspection Service presented a report to the Education Committee entitled 'Education and Attitudes'. The report was based on work carried out in Nottinghamshire schools between June 1988 and May 1989 and stemmed from the Education Committee's interest in multi-cultural education, equal opportunities and pastoral care in schools. The foreword to the report stated:

> In conducting this review we took as our starting point the assumption that education cannot be value or attitude free. The belief which underpinned the review was that schools have a responsibility to empower pupils to develop, express and refine their own values and attitudes. A central purpose was to examine how schools approach this work. In particular we were concerned to understand how schools' practices reflect and develop values and attitudes which promote equal opportunities for all.

Having received the report, the Committee considered that the issues raised were of such fundamental importance that further examination was necessary if the recommendations contained in it were to be implemented effectively by schools. With this in mind, a Panel of elected members was established to undertake this task, supported by Education Department Officers and members of the Advisory and

Inspection Service. The Panel included members of all three political groups and teacher representatives on the Education Committee. The Panel was chaired by the Chairman of the Education Committee, Councillor Fred Riddell.

The final report of the Members' Panel was approved by the Education Committee in November 1990 and distributed in a published form to all schools in Nottinghamshire and to other interested parties.

The Panel looked in detail at the Report's main theme of the relationship between the process of education and the development of attitudes by pupils. The original Advisory and Inspection Service Report contained more than 40 recommendations of ways in which schools can address this relationship in a practical way at a whole school level. At a more specific level, bullying, gender and racial attacks and harassment were felt to be particular areas of concern to schools. The Panel produced guidelines and possible action plans to help schools develop responses to these difficult problems. These guidelines were based on examples of existing good practice to be found in Nottinghamshire schools and others drawn from previously produced research and literature.

The work on bullying undertaken by the Authority therefore needs to be seen in this context and the remainder of this chapter is in 2 parts: firstly, a summary analysis of the research undertaken and, secondly, an Action Checklist for Nottinghamshire schools. This Checklist is firmly rooted in the summary analysis and seeks to encourage schools to address bullying as a whole school issue. Both parts appear in the form in which they appeared in the Members' Panel's final report.

Bullying – a whole school issue

1. Introduction

1.1 There are numerous definitions of exactly what constitutes 'bullying' although most only vary in their choice of words rather than in what they are trying to convey.

1.2 Bullying is generally taken to mean any sort of systematic physical or psychological intimidation and may be easy to detect or take more subtle forms.

1.3 What is more important than the definition, however, is the effect that bullying can have on:

(a) the victims who often already suffer from a poor self image.

(b) the bullies for whom such behaviour may lead to other forms of anti-social activity.

1.4 One aspect of bullying which warrants separate attention is the connection between bullying and racial harassment. While this form of bullying has certain similarities with other types, there are also some fundamental differences and this particular aspect of the problem requires separate attention.

1.5 In the past there has been a tendency to treat bullying as almost a 'natural' phenomenon or 'part of growing up'. There has often been a reluctance on the part of pupils to report incidents of bullying because it has not been seen as a whole school issue and they do not perceive consistency among staff in dealing with the issue.

2. Research

2.1 Much of the research into the causes, effects and methods of dealing with bullying has been undertaken as part of broader studies into discipline and ways of dealing with disruptive behaviour.

2.2 Strategies for dealing with bullying are often written into individual school documents dealing with codes of conduct and behaviour and there do not appear to be many Local Education Authorities which have taken a lead in publishing guidelines for their institutions.

2.3 Certain common themes emerge from the research which has been undertaken into bullying:

(a) about 1 in 4 children are involved in bullying, either as bullies or victims,

(b) cases of bullying generally last for 12 months or more,

(c) both bullies and victims tend to have poor curriculum attainment and are less popular with teaching staff,

(d) although it is important to avoid behaviour stereotyping and bullying manifests itself in many ways, much of that which occurs between boys focuses on physical aggression and violence, whilst girls employ planned verbal techniques, such as spreading rumours and 'sending to Coventry',

(e) most bullying happens in the same class and year group,

(f) school break times are often the flashpoints for bullying and a time of great anxiety for many children,

(g) the other major times when incidents occur are on the way to and from school and these too can be times of great stress for children, particularly as there is frequently no adult supervision at all.

2.4 Any attempt to reduce bullying is made more difficult in that bullying is often the most immediate manifestation of endemic social problems. Research into bullying makes clear:

    (a) that both victims and bullies are three times as likely as other children to be experiencing significant domestic difficulties,

    (b) that bullying is related to negative gender images,

    (c) that ethnic origin is often a significant factor in bullying,

    (d) that the incidence of bullying is consistently higher in areas of social deprivation.

2.5 The social context for bullying is compounded by the complex roles experienced:

    (a) in one fifth of cases bullying is provoked by victims, whose interpersonal skills and self image stimulate aggression in others,

    (b) one in five bullies can be classed as 'anxious bullies', who are suffering major educational difficulties,

    (c) in some cases, assertive and provocative behaviour by children can result in them ending up both as victims and bullies,

    (d) if patterns of bullying are not challenged within a school, they can become ingrained in the 'culture' of the institution and thus self perpetuating. An example of this would be 'initiation ceremonies' which new pupils are expected to take part in by older pupils.

3. Responses to bullying

3.1 School discipline is consistently identified by parents as a major issue in evaluating their local schools. In one Authority, 'customer research' has shown that parents rate discipline as second only to good tuition in deciding what makes a good secondary school. Amongst parents in that Authority concerned about discipline, 70% rated bullying as a key issue.

3.2 Given this level of concern, the political profile of discipline is inevitable and in many cases the Elton Report is seen as a watershed in policy. The thrust of the Elton Report, however, is the enabling of teachers to cope better with discipline problems.

3.3 In many cases, bullying happens simply because teachers do not know about it. It is, therefore, important that any strategies to counter bullying centre on both preventative measures and enabling children to deal better with problems as they arise.

3.4 The Elton Report stated that:

An important factor in promoting good behaviour among pupils is a curriculum which they see as being relevant to their needs.

Clearly, the implementation of the Education Committee's Curriculum Statement, with its emphasis on entitlement and relevance, and curriculum developments (e.g. TVEI and the Record of Achievement scheme) in the 14–16 age group are positive steps in promoting behaviour.

3.5 In addition to the broad curriculum, there is evidence that bullying is reduced where schools take a series of internal steps:

- making bullying an explicit theme, both within school management planning and as part of the PSE curriculum.
- researching bullying within the school, both formally and informally, and pursuing consequent monitoring arrangements.
- targeting supervision arrangements on times and places where bullying may occur.
- tackling bullying patterns particularly in the first year group of the school.

4. A partnership approach

4.1 Perhaps the real key to tackling school discipline in general and bullying in particular is the careful fostering of a partnership between pupils, parents, teachers, Governors and the Education Committee.

4.2 Most research indicates the key role of parental involvement in anti-bullying strategies. Manchester Education Committee has suggested a number of steps in increasing parental involvement as part of improving discipline:

- a greater number of less formal parents' evenings.
- 'open days', at least once a term, where parents can go anywhere in the school throughout a working day.
- the allocation of accommodation to be available to parents and groups of parents at all times.

4.3 In the end, bullying concerns the relationship between children, but it also happens in an environment where children understand that what is happening is wrong and could lead to punishment of some sort. Research on discipline has repeatedly shown that children request a consistent approach to discipline within a school and, furthermore, that there is a need to develop rewards as well as sanctions in any discipline policy. In their report on 'Good Behaviour and Discipline in School', HMI commented that:

The balance between rewards and sanctions ... is a useful touchstone of a school's approach to maintaining good standards of behaviour. The best results are found where schools lay particular emphasis on rewards.

4.4 Research on bullying issues indicates a number of pupil-centred approaches which can be followed:

- an agreed code of conduct, which makes clear what good behaviour is and how it will be rewarded, along with a description of unacceptable behaviour and the sanctions which will follow. Such a code of conduct would be agreed by Governors, implemented by school staff and distributed to all parents and pupils,
- the creation of rewards for good behaviour, which would build upon the philosophy of the Committee's Record of Achievement, and which would foster responsibility and co-operation leading to privileges and public recognition,
- a representative forum (e.g. a pupil council) for pupils, which can pursue issues of behaviour,
- holistic approaches to dealing with triggers to bullying – e.g., personal hygiene, non-local accents, etc. – throughout the curriculum,
- developing curricular and pastoral services within a school which can deal with the complexities of bullying, e.g. supporting an 'anxious bully',
- recognising that some pupils feel bullied by certain teachers and creating situations where pupils feel free to be candid about this,
- introducing structured activities into break times which increase supervision and further co-operative activities at the same time as minimising individual isolation,
- the introduction of male midday supervisors (e.g. retired men) who can supervise difficult areas such as boys' toilets.

4.5 The Education Committee has a key role within this partnership:

- the production of detailed guidelines for schools on both the importance of anti-bullying strategies and the key features which such schemes should include,
- developing a consultancy role for schools through the Education Welfare Service, Educational Psychology Service, the Advisory and Inspection Service and the Nottinghamshire Educational Support Service,
- leading an INSET programme both for school Governors and for staff concerned with pastoral care,
- reviewing the deployment of existing resources, e.g. mid-day supervisors,
- producing anti-bullying materials, for both classroom and pastoral uses, which are targeted at a variety of specific audiences, e.g. parents, pupils.

5. Next steps

5.1 This paper identified:

- some features of bullying which arise from the research in this area,
- a range of possible first steps, which the Committee might wish to recommend to schools,
- the need for a partnership approach in tackling this problem and consequently the need for schools to produce and implement policies which follow on from developmental work in schools, such as that in two Nottinghamshire comprehensive schools which has been featured in the local press.

5.2 As a contribution to this process the 'Action Checklist for Schools' was produced by the Panel and this forms the remainder of this chapter.

AN ACTION CHECKLIST FOR NOTTINGHAMSHIRE SCHOOLS

Senior management team

1. Making bullying an explicit theme

○ What do we currently know about bullying in the school?
○ Have we made a clear statement about bullying and how we deal with

it? Should this statement be available to the Governors and all staff, pupils and parents?

○ Should we include bullying as an issue in our curriculum and management planning?

○ Is it important to begin a developmental process of understanding more about bullying in the school? Should this lead to bullying becoming an important whole-school issue and to solutions which are consistent with our curricular and pastoral aims?

2. *Finding out more about bullying*

○ Do we need any external consultancy in beginning a debate on bullying as a whole school issue?

○ Should we adopt some formal methods of researching the problem? Would a confidential questionnaire for pupils be a good idea? Should the problem be explored and measured by classroom debate?

○ Whether or not we follow a structured programme of researching the problem, should we establish a formal monitoring system to log incidents of bullying?

3. *A code of conduct?*

○ Do we have an agreed code of conduct?

○ If we have a code of conduct or are planning to have one, does it clearly identify bullying and does it establish consistent procedures for dealing with the problem?

○ Does our code of conduct make clear what good behaviour is and how it will be rewarded, along with a description of unacceptable behaviour and the sanctions which will follow?

○ Is the code of conduct a written document agreed by the Governing Body and circulated to all pupils and parents? Is it part of our school brochure?

4. *Present pastoral arrangements*

○ Do our present pastoral arrangements effectively tackle personal difficulties faced by individual pupils at an early enough stage to prevent such difficulties leading to symptomatic bullying problems? Are our pastoral resources strained at times in dealing with symptoms, rather than underlying problems?

○ Should we make clear to all pupils that bullying should be reported to any member of staff and that whoever takes the report will act immediately?

- ○ Should all reports, however minor the incident seems, be logged centrally so that trends and particular problems can be detected quickly?
- ○ How could we establish an effective follow-up system to any report of bullying? How could we 'track' bullies and victims, without increasing difficulties for pupils involved?
- ○ Is it likely that, for whatever reasons, some pupils feel bullied at times by particular teachers? How can pupils candidly raise such difficulties with other members of staff? How would staff react if such reports were treated seriously by senior managers?
- ○ How can pupils be encouraged to accept pastoral responsibility for other pupils?

5. Encouraging pupils to share ownership of any solutions

- ○ Do we have a representative forum for pupils, where they can consider issues of behaviour? How might a 'pupil council' help in identifying and solving bullying problems?
- ○ Do pupils feel that discipline follows an agreed and consistent policy, in terms of procedures, rewards and sanctions?
- ○ Is there sufficient emphasis on bullying as an issue in the First Year to act against the cultural momentum of bullying becoming an accepted part of school life?
- ○ Would a 'bully book', logging incidents of bullying, be a useful deterrent sanction?
- ○ Do pupils have their own publications in which to pursue the issue of bullying?
- ○ What sort of pastoral roles could pupils assume for themselves?

6. Parental involvement

- ○ Do parents understand the school's code of conduct?
- ○ Do parents have confidence that bullying is treated seriously and do they know how the school is attempting to minimise the problem?
- ○ When we identify bullying in the school, at what stage should the parents of both bullies and victims be contacted? What is expected of parents at various stages? Should such expectations be made clear to all parents?
- ○ Is it possible to improve communication and partnership between school and parents on discipline issues? Would more frequent, less formal meetings with parents be more effective?
- ○ Would the presence of parents about the school improve discipline? Is there any spare accommodation that could be made available for

parent use? Would open days each term be possible, where parents can go anywhere in the school on an ordinary working day?

O In particular cases, where rewards and sanctions are being considered should a pupil's parents be involved in deciding on appropriate measures?

O Should we use any of our incentive allowances for home-school liaison?

7. *Improving supervision*

O When bullying, however subtle, happens in the classroom, do teachers act consistently in dealing with it?

O Can we identify 'flashpoints' in the school and during the day when bullying is more likely? How could we target supervision on these problems?

O Is it possible to increase the role of structured activities in break-times?

O How effective are our Mid-day Supervisors? Is there a need for training for MDS's? Would employing some male MDS's (e.g. early retired men) increase the overall effectiveness?

O Are there any aspects of the school's physical design or use which reduce the effectiveness of supervision?

O Is there any system for collecting feedback from non-school staff (e.g. bus drivers, school-crossing staff) on supervision problems?

Curriculum leaders

1. *Implementing a curricular approach to dealing with bullying*

O To what extent should bullying lead to a cross-curricular approach and to what extent should it be dealt with separately in PSE?

O In a cross-curricular approach, to what extent do existing themes discourage bullying?

O Could bullying be approached through a spiral structure, both in terms of curricular themes and as a discrete issue?

O If bullying gained a high profile in the curriculum, would the pastoral and management approaches to bullying be responsive to the outcomes of classroom work?

2. *Cross-curricular issues*

O How is co-operation promoted both as a theme and a process throughout the curriculum?

O Does bullying, amongst both boys and girls, often result from negative gender images? How are these dealt with in the curriculum?

○ Is there any evidence that ethnicity and culture are factors in bullying? Is the multi-cultural curriculum dealing successfully with the sort of issues involved in bullying incidents?

○ Does the curriculum develop a sense of responsibility for a pupil's own actions and for acting positively when another pupil is experiencing difficulty?

3. Whole curriculum planning

○ What systems of reward and sanction exist within the curriculum?

○ What has been learnt from recent initiatives (e.g. RoA's, TVEI) in making the curriculum more relevant to pupils, which would impact on improving both behaviour and pupils' sense of attainment?

○ Are both general and specific learning difficulties catered for across the school? Is the provision sensitive to some of the causes of bullying e.g. disaffection, labelling as 'weak'?

○ When particular individuals are identified as bullies or victims, what remedial solutions exist within the curriculum?

○ To what extent does the school structure an informal curriculum e.g. could an anti-bullying strategy develop within extra-curricular activities?

4. Particular themes related to bullying

○ How can bullying be dealt with specifically? Should it be delivered in a spiral approach throughout the school?

○ How could underlying issues, like aggression, be dealt with?

○ How would we introduce the complexity of the issue e.g. the role of the anxious bully?

○ What is the best way to develop the confidence of pupils to handle threatening situations and to intervene/report when they know that another pupil is feeling threatened?

○ How can classroom work be channelled into the whole-school approach, encouraging pupils to feel a sense of ownership of any solution?

INSET for all staff

1. Terms of reference

○ What are the plans of the senior management team and curriculum leaders for dealing with bullying?

○ Do we wish to use an outside consultant as a facilitator?

○ What do we mean by bullying and where would any plans for dealing with it fit into our current priorities?

○ Is this an issue for which all staff have an equal responsibility or would it be more effective to identify key players in any development?

○ What other whole school issues have we dealt with through INSET and what lessons did we learn about progressing such issues?

2. Reviewing experience

○ Do we have a common definition of bullying and should all incidents be treated seriously?

○ How does bullying relate to issues of equal opportunities?

○ Is bullying at this school any different to that at other schools?

○ Are we confident in handling bullying situations?

○ What kind of reward and sanction systems have we employed?

○ Can we identify how far we are consistent in dealing with bullying?

3. Challenging our own practice

○ Are there any aspects of our own practice, which might produce some of the more complex bully/victim roles e.g. are there pupils who are clearly not liked by teachers?

○ Can we recognise any situations where certain pupils might feel bullied by a member of staff?

○ Are there times when we are not conscious of less obvious bullying e.g. name-calling, sending to Coventry?

○ Do we ever condone bullying by not challenging it?

○ When we do challenge bullying, are we sure that our challenges are effective?

○ Are we happy for there to be clear routes for pupils to complain when they feel bullied by a particular teacher? Would you be willing to not be defensive if a pupil complained about you?

4. Curricular change

○ Is the school planning to deal with bullying through cross-curricular themes, specific subject areas or a mixture of both?

○ Is such a curricular strategy of themes and subjects underpinned by an appropriate learning process, which fosters an environment for change?

○ How would the profile of bullying in the curriculum impact on your own teaching programmes? How would you measure the effectiveness of including bullying in the curriculum?

5. Pastoral care

- ○ How will the school's proposals to manage change in pastoral care work in practice?
- ○ How might informal pastoral roles be developed to encourage pupils to be open about bullying?
- ○ How would you develop pupils' own responsibility for pastoral care?

The way forward

The Panel's report was circulated to all schools in the Authority and three major uses were envisaged for it. Firstly, as an information resource identifying good practice and effective strategies; secondly, as a source of support for school self-review; and thirdly, as a source of support in identifying strategies for change.

In order to provide further support, the members of the Inspection Team involved with the preparation and publication of the original report have been involved in supporting in-service training events organised by schools and families of schools. Looking at the ways in which schools seek to develop attitudes and values in pupils has also come to be part of the normal process of inspection and support in schools.

While the report represents the culmination of the Panel's work, it has provided a starting point for some schools and a contribution towards work already under way in others.

CHAPTER 12

Limiting Bullying in Residential Care

Norman Elliot and David Thompson

Some children or young people stay in residential care, for example in residential schools for emotionally and behaviourally disturbed children, children's homes, or other establishments providing residential training. Such a residential community is not just a school or training establishment with living rooms attached, although it may seem so to the outsider. Residential living means that the whole personality of the student is involved in the community, and that the relationships set up in the community and the attitudes and skills learnt by the students have much more impact, for better or worse, than in a non-residential setting. Bullying inside such a community actively poisons the supportive relationships aimed for by the staff, and indicates that the basic emotional structure of the community is threatened.

What needs do the young people have?

Children and young people in a residential community usually have special needs of some degree, and the structure and organisation of the community is aimed to meet those needs as effectively as possible. The basic responsibility of the adults is to give the affection, care and structure to enable the young people to learn effectively, and the type of structure arrived at has to be designed to meet the special needs of the youngsters. However, many communities have to include young people with a range of needs, which often means that they have to have worked out clearly what needs of children they are able to meet, and what structures and patterns of organisation are necessary to achieve that. These patterns include the various policies and procedures for setting standards of social behaviour and maintaining control, as far as that is necessary. Bullying is an example of one of a range of very unwelcome activities by which people reject and discriminate against each other, others being racism and sexism, which the community has to reject through the leadership of its staff.

To achieve this, procedures have to be planned. Typically, such procedures would include:

(1) Well described discipline policies, which all staff understand and keep to.

(2) Non-punitive sanctions wherever possible, to avoid institutionalising aggressive interpersonal relationships.

(3) Well defined boundaries for what is allowed and what is not allowed, which the young people understand, with clear rewards and clear sanctions.

(4) Good communications systems between children and staff and between staff.

(5) Clear support systems for staff.

Complications arise in residential settings, because if children, or groups of children, have different needs, their boundaries, sanctions, rewards, and communication systems may be different. The community's procedures have to be sufficiently flexible and specific to meet these different needs. If this is not so, then gradually the community will slide to a position where it is ignoring the needs of some group of young people, and the process of institutionalisation will begin. Communication between children and staff will reduce, and conditions for bullying to occur will appear.

Resisting creeping institutionalisation

Communities have to recognise that they can easily turn into institutions, and actively work against the institutionalising processes which gradually depersonalise young people. The control exercised should be the minimum control necessary for the young people to grow and learn for themselves, and in practice this is achieved much more easily if there is sufficient homogeneity within the groups or subgroups. Totally individualised curricula may be the ideal, but this requires a staffiing ratio much better than most schools or communities have, and needs have to be met on many occasions by grouping young persons together and treating them as a group. In this way the degree of control by adults can be varied from almost total to minimal, and in the latter case the young people have a real chance of learning some of the ways that a group can establish high standards of behaviour itself. The 'silent majority' of young people prefer that bullying is not a part of their world, and given clear adult leadership that it is possible to establish co-operative relationships in their friend-ships groups, will do so. Some young people will still dominate others, but the essential elements of persistent aggression on an obviously weaker person to achieve dominance need not be there. The leaders of the group achieve their position through genuine leadership skills.

Introducing new members

When a community is running effectively, new children joining it need to be introduced to its standards quickly. The admissions policy should be clearly known, so that staff can easily include the newcomer into existing groups without undue strain on the groups concerned. At this stage, some communities would discuss aspects of behaviour expected with the newcomer as part of the induction process, and may work on a specific contract between the young person and the community. This would specify what the community would do for the young person, as well as what they would do for the group. The specific agreement to no alcohol, no drugs, and no violence might be the beginning of such a contract. The detailed anti-bullying provisions in the community would then be structured to avoid the isolation of any victim by stressing accessibility of staff and their desire and capacity to help, building up the pattern of positive relationships with all the young people to support that communication, allowing ample time for staff to communicate with each other on a day to day basis about the stresses affecting the youngsters, and including time in the timetable for discussion and other explorations of relationships. The normal life of the community would also lead to children forming positive relationships with each other which did not involve bullying and other forms of systematic rejection.

Young people in residential settings still have parents, and they should be involved if their children are either bullies or victims. Some parents under stress, or who hold very punitive attitudes to their children, may be able to do very little to help, but others may be able to add their weight to that of the community in an appropriate way.

Quality in supervision

One of the remedies for bullying frequently advised, and frequently appropriately used, is increased supervision of those situations where it might occur. Where children have specific identified needs, the quality of the supervision is important. This means not merely stopping bullying occurring if it is seen, but in general being aware of the needs of the children in that particular setting and intervening when necessary to see that they are met. Staff also need skills in handling conflict resolution among young people, and in distinguishing when conflicts are 'play' and when they are for real. Supervision is also necessary overnight, as anxieties and tensions in children often arise at bedtime. Knowing that a friendly adult is always available, and awake, throughout the night, is both a support to a potential victim and a deterrent to a potential bully.

In the last resort, however, the community has to have the option of excluding from its membership any young person whom the community fails to stop persistently bullying. Before this, other physical measures such as separating the bully from his victims will have been tried and failed, but the eventual responsibility of the adults to maintain the emotional cohesion of the community has to include the possibility of exclusion. This could be seen as a last stage in the demonstration to the bully of the rejection by the community of his behaviour, leading to a contract with him for return on specific conditions. In any case, the adults still have the responsibility to the bully to provide for his needs, and alternative provision should be ready.

Staff support

As can be seen, stopping bullying depends on staff implementing well thought out supportive, educational, and disciplinary procedures consistently. Staff need support and training to do this, and constant encouragement to communicate with each other and with the young people. Induction, appropriate training opportunities, and appraisal are all ways of providing that support, which also allow for different staff to have different levels of conceptualisation of the problem. Staff in residential settings often come from a range of backgrounds, and their conceptualisations of care, control, discipline, and bullying will be different from each other. Providing that the internal discussions result in an agreed set of principles and procedures, such differences are not disadvantages.

Where are the limits?

Bullying often occurs in residential settings when the 'ideal' conditions described above are not met, usually through deficiencies in management and resourcing which result in great stress on staff, or through inadequate or ignored admissions policies. If the community is under pressure to take in another young person because this is the only place available, rather than because this placement can meet their needs, the internal care and control systems come under increasing strain. The strain leads to breakdown in relationships and a greater probability of bullying. Ultimately, measures to reduce bullying need political support with the will to allocate resources. Goodwill, good training and support and good management can only go so far.

CHAPTER 13

The Prevention of Bullying among Incarcerated Delinquents

Barry J. McGurk and Cynthia McDougall

This chapter describes events which are somewhat historical as they relate to bullying which occurred some time ago in the borstal system. The borstal system has since been superseded by Youth Custody and more recently by the Unified Custodial Sentence. Also, the dormitory conditions at the borstal in question now no longer exist. The information is, however, relevant to current problems, as it describes the bullying which can arise when young people are contained in unsupervised dormitory conditions, and the measures which can be taken to contain the bullying problem.

Criminological literature on bullying in British residential institutions for young offenders is, as far as the authors are aware, nonexistent. In America, the classic studies of Polsky (1962) and Feld (1977) have concentrated on describing the establishment of seemingly inescapable social systems within inmate groupings which led to 'scapegoats' being dominated and humiliated by other inmates higher up the hierarchy. This paper aims to contribute to the literature by describing the nature and extent of bullying in a British penal institution for young offenders, the efforts made by the Prison Department to reduce the problem, and an evaluation of the relative success of these efforts.

Combating bullying can be seen as falling within the scope of the general rubric of 'situational crime prevention' as defined by Clarke

(1983). The behaviour labelled as bullying breaks specific, institutionalised, codes of conduct (Prison Rules). The measures used to combat the problem involve the management of the immediate environment in order to reduce the opportunities for bullying and increase the likelihood of detection.

The study commenced in November 1979 when the authors were asked by the Governor of a Borstal which we will call 'Riverdale', a custodial institution for appoximately 300 young offenders age 15-21 years, in England, to look into bullying activities which he suspected occurred in the dormitory accommodation provided for the majority of inmates. 180 of the inmates were located on the site of an ex-army camp in 10 dormitories; 18 inmates per dormitory. Each dormitory was housed in a physically separate, rectangular, single storey building. Inmates were locked in the dormitories overnight from late evening to early morning. A member of staff did not reside in each dormitory, and as such, inmates were unsupervised except for visits from night patrol officers at intervals throughout the night. Each dormitory had one exit/entrance via locked doors. Anyone approaching a dormitory from any direction could be seen from the windows at a distance of 20-50 yards. A further 120 inmates were located in two purpose-built blocks in individual cells.

All inmates having spent approximately one-third of their sentence in the cellular accommodation were then allocated to the dormitories – regardless of offence, body build or psychological make up.

Hence the Governor's concern as the conditions for bullying to occur existed par excellence. The institution had the highest proportion of dormitory accommodation among British penal establishments. The dormitories were virtually unsupervised (and unsupervisable) at night, with unselected groups of delinquents occupying them. Yet an examination of the previous 100 offences against discipline committed by inmates revealed that only *one* offence involved bullying. Both the perceived risk, and actual risk of being apprehended, were therefore very low.

Method

The approach adopted was to interview individually as many randomly chosen inmates as the two authors could see independently in a single 2 hour session – the period during which the vast majority of inmates attended morning, educationally based, classes. An inmate was chosen for interview, taken from his class, interviewed, but not allowed to return to his class following interview in order to avoid contamination effects. Twenty-three inmates were interviewed. By way of introduction we explained to the inmates that we were 'outsiders' who worked at a nearby Remand Centre (which was 35 miles away). At the Remand Centre we had talked to ex-Riverdale inmates who had been reconvicted and arrived back in the prison system at the Remand Centre. These individuals had told us about the bullying occurring at Riverdale. (This had in fact happened). In other words we implied that we *knew* that bullying occurred. We were simply interested in determining the extent and nature of it. We also told the inmates we did not wish to know about specific incidents nor any of the names of inmates involved in bullying. We structured the brief interviews so that each inmate was asked the same questions.

This crude, relatively simple and unsophisticated method was adopted to determine the nature and extent of bullying. A package of situationally focussed measures to combat the problem was then introduced. Following that the interview procedure was repeated periodically, different inmates each time, to determine the efficacy of the measures.

Initial assessment of bullying

The extent of bullying

Fourteen of the 23 inmates said that they had witnessed bullying at least once in the last week. Five of the inmates had only heard about the bullying at Riverdale and four said they had not seen bullying nor heard about bullying at Riverdale during the previous week.

The nature of bullying

There appeared to be an inmate culture at Riverdale dominated by various techniques of bullying. These techniques, which sometimes had curious names, are listed below:

(1) A 'Tetley' – a trainee, naked except for a pair of underpants on his head, with a broomstick in his hand, sings a song (usually the 'Tetley Tea Bag' song from a TV advert) and dances round the dormitory. Sometimes the inmate is tied to a bed and a broomstick is pushed into his rectum.

(2) A 'Kestrel' – a cup of water is placed on the pillow of a sleeping inmate and a boot is thrown at him. His startled response spills the water on his pillow and face.

(3) An 'Eagle' – a fire bucket full of water is placed on the bedside locker of a sleeping inmate and a boot is thrown at it, knocking it over onto the inmate.

(4) A 'Whodunit' – a blanket is thrown over the head of a trainee and the other trainees hit him with sticks or kick him.

(5) Dormitory 'Death' Runs – an initiation ceremony for new dormitory members in which the new trainee runs the gauntlet of inmates who hit them with pillowcases, some of which contain boots.

(6) A trainee is held down or tied to a bed and his testicles are covered in boot black and polished.

(7) Shaving an inmate's pubic hair whilst tied to a bed.

(8) Mock Hangings – inmates are 'hung' from windows or threatened with being pushed off the top of a bed which is stood on end. A noose is placed round their neck which is attached to the top of the bed.

(9) Paper is placed between inmates toes and set on fire.

(10) Petrol is poured over inmates feet and they are threatened that it will be set on fire.

(11) Drinking urine.

(12) 'Rape' – originally we thought this to be homosexual rape but in the light of subsequent information we believed that this was a situation in which a naked trainee is beaten with slippers.

(13) Masturbating another trainee.

(14) Receiving a beating if a trainee is unable to pay debts, is thought to be a 'Grass' or who refuses to be a 'Joey' (do the chores of another inmate).

(15) An enforced type of breathing and shaking of the head that results in loss of consciousness.

Where did bullying occur?

Eighteen of the 19 inmates who had seen/heard about bullying said that it happened in the dormitories. Four of these inmates also said that they had seen inmates beaten at work. One inmate said he knew of someone who had been beaten in the cellular accommodation.

When did bullying occur?

Tuesday evenings (new members of the dormitory arrived on Tuesday) and Friday evenings (dormitories were not inspected Saturday mornings) were mentioned by trainees as popular times for bullying.

How often did bullying occur?

Out of the trainees who had witnessed bullying, estimates varied from 'non-stop every night, sometimes all night' to 'mainly Tuesdays and Fridays'. Certainly an 'averaged opinion' suggest a frequency of bullying of about every other night.

Preventative measures

Following the initial assessment of bullying the authors discussed preventative measures with representative groups of prison staff at the institution. This ad hoc consultative approach resulted in the adoption over a period of three months of an anti-bullying package by the Governor. During this time the major measures which were implemented were:

(1) An Assistant Governor was given managerial responsibility for the dormitory units, and at least one visit at night to the dormitory area by a Governor grade was made each week.

(2) A light switch operating the lights inside each dormitory was placed on the *outside* wall of each dormitory block next to the entrance door and hence a night patrol officer could turn on the dormitory lights without having to go through the time-consuming and noisy business of opening doors with keys, in order to enter a dormitory to turn the lights on. With such a switch outside the dormitory the officer could turn the light on and view the inside of the dormitory quicker than previously if he suspected misbehaviour within.

(3) Televisions (colour) were located in each dormitory to combat boredom.

(4) Differential allocation on reception to either the dormitories or cells was commenced. Inmates thought 'unsuitable', on an intuitive basis, (such as those with a history of violence or previous bullying offences) were not allocated to the dormitory accommodation.

(5) The Night Patrol's routines were restructured in an attempt to vary the timing of visits to the dormitory area, and giving more time patrolling the dormitory area of the prison than the cell blocks.

(6) Body checks on inmates were made by prison staff every morning to detect injuries. Inmates were told to strip to their underpants and their bodies were examined for tissue damage.

(7) Problem check lists were included in the assessment techniques used within the first week of arrival in order to allow inmates to communicate, without having to approach a member of staff directly, any problems they were suffering.

(8) Two Prison Auxiliaries (a supporting grade to Prison Officers) were employed in day-time patrol duties in order to allow staff to interact more with trainees to discuss problems.

(9) Training sessions for staff were carried out to increase, for example,

vigilance among night patrols and interrogation skills among staff interviewing inmates suspected of being involved as perpetrators in bullying incidents.

(10) Severe penalties for offences involving bullying were awarded.

(11) The problem would be monitored regularly by the authors.

These relatively simple expedients were designed to increase (a) the surveillance by staff of the problem, (b) the risk of being apprehended, and (c) the punishment incurred when caught.

Reassessments of bullying

Folllowing the initial assessment in December 1979, reassessments took place in April 1980 and July 1980. Our findings were as follows:

The extent of bullying

The number of positive responses to the question, 'Have you seen any bullying during the last week?' were:

December 1979	April 1980	July 1980
14 out of 23 inmates	12 out of 23 inmates	3 out of 23 inmates

The number of positive responses to the question, 'Have you heard about any bullying happening during the last week?' were:

December 1979	April 1980	July 1980
5 out of 23 inmates	4 out of 23 inmates	10 out of 23 inmates

There is a statistically significant (chi-square = 11.54, $p < .005$) decrease in the number of inmates reporting having seen bullying in the last week. There is also an increase (though not statistically significant; chi-square = 5.44, $p < .10$) in the number of inmates hearing about bullying, but this was largely due to inmates talking to each other about one particular bullying incident which was detected by staff two weeks before our visit in July 1980.

The nature of bullying: April 1980

Techniques of bullying were again elicited from the inmates at our reassessment of the problem in April 1980. The list is very similar to the list described earlier with some subtle though important differences. 'Tetleys', 'Kestrels', 'Whodunits', 'Dorm Runs', and burning paper between inmates toes were mentioned as commonly occurring but the perverted and dangerous aspects of these techniques were *not* evident. For example, a 'Tetley' (a trainee naked except for a pair of underpants on his head, with broomstick in hand, sings a song) no longer concluded with the broomstick being pushed into the inmate's rectum. Dorm runs no longer involved pillowcases full of boots; they involved simply pillows. In addition, the explicitly dangerous techniques (e.g. mock hangings, petrol on feet) and sexual techniques (e.g. shaving pubic hair, enforced masturbation) appeared to have virtually ceased in the dormitories.

Some techniques we had not heard about previously were described – 'Moon Job' (an inmate's bed is stood on end while he's asleep and he slides out of bed); a 'Crocodile' – an inmate is bitten by other inmates; and an 'Octopus' – a bucket of human waste, is emptied over an inmate. A further method of inducing unconsciousness – a 'Buzz' – was described. The carotid artery in the neck is physically blocked by a stranglehold from another inmate until unconsciousness results. Of all the techniques of bullying identified in April 1980 this would appear to be the most dangerous as it could *easily* lead to brain damage or death. It should be pointed out, however, that the inmates were probably unaware of the danger of a 'Buzz'.

Where, when and how often did bullying occur: April 1980

Most of the trainees said that the dormitories were the main focus for bullying although some inmates mentioned the 'Joiners' as being the focus for boot blacking (of the genital area) when a trainee left the Joiners. According to the inmates, the most popular times for bullying were Friday and Saturday nights (after TV finishes) and late Sunday afternoons (when TV is uninteresting to inmates because of the religious programmes). Estimates of how often bullying occurred varied from 'not very often at all' to 'every weekend'.

The average length of time the interviewed inmates had been in the dormitories was 8 weeks and the majority of measures in the anti bullying package were introduced within this period. Consequently we were able to ask the inmates whether the bullying was worse/better/about the same as it was when they first arrived in the dormitories. Seventeen out of 23 inmates said it was 'better' than when they first arrived in the dormitories (12 trainees put the improvement down to TVs, the remainder to heavier punishments and body checks). Two inmates said it was 'about the same'. Three inmates 'didn't know' as they hadn't been in the dormitories long enough to notice any changes. One inmate said it had always been 'OK'.

The nature of bullying: July 1980

All of the inmates had heard of 'Tetleys', 'Kestrels' etc. but as is shown above, only three inmates had witnessed bullying in the last week, and these incidents all involved inmates being 'pushed around' for not acting as a 'Joey' (doing jobs for other inmates) or for not handing over tobacco or money for tobacco. Two inmates reported recently, though not in the last week, having seen enforced masturbation and oral sex, and one inmate reported having seen a 'Kangaroo Court' and 'Dorm Run'.

Where, when and how often did bullying occur: July 1980

Inmates' bullying occurred infrequently in the dormitories, at night, or on Sunday afternoons. The frequency of bullying appeared to have decreased significantly. Most inmates said that it didn't happen at all. Interestingly, three of the inmates had been in Riverdale during 1979 and all three said that the bullying situation had changed considerably. They indicated a dramatic reduction in the extent of the bullying.

Discussion

A number of points need to be made about the methodology adopted to assess the bullying problem at Riverdale as the rigour usually associated with sound social science investigations is lacking. We adopted the strategy of asking a small sample of inmates whether they had seen or heard about bullying during the previous week, without asking for information on specific incidents. We could not ask for the names of inmates involved in incidents when these incidents had not been detected by staff. If we had asked for details we would not have received information as we would have been asking inmates to break the unwritten rule against informing on fellow inmates. Whilst our strategy led us to receive a great deal of information, we did not have specific details relating to incidents and we could not directly cross-check them. Hence we did not know whether inmates were exaggerating, or playing down, the problem.

Indirect corroboration, however, of the nature and extent of bullying came from two main sources. Firstly, following discussions on the problem with the Governor and senior staff, numerous incidents, of an identical nature to those described by inmates to the authors, began to be detected by staff. Secondly, with the introduction of the anti-bullying measures a significant reduction in injuries occurring among inmates in the dormitories was reported when the last three months of 1979 were contrasted with the first three months of 1980.

Further to the assessments and reassessments of the problem reported here, similar reassessments of bullying at Riverdale occurred in February and May 1981 prior to the scheduled closing of the old army-style dormitories as new purpose built cell blocks became available. Over this period bullying returned to numerically equivalent levels as in our first assessment of the problem but with two important differences. Firstly, dangerous and perverted activities were not reported by inmates and were not brought to the attention of staff. Secondly, the less serious forms of bullying occurred equally as much in the cellular accommodation as in the dormitories. In May 1981, for example inmates reported that 'Kestrels' occurred in the dormitories but 'Joeying' and being beaten for being unable to repay borrowed tobacco occurred in the cellular accommodation. Virtually all the activities being reported to us by inmates were now being detected by staff and being dealt with by the Governor.

In comparison with other crime prevention initiatives, the prevention of bullying in a total institution should be a simple endeavour, given the relatively high level of control of the environment afforded to those implementing the programme. However as Hall and Baker (1973) reported when they introduced a token economy programme in a psychiatric hospital, the most crucial factor affecting success is the attitude of staff toward the programme, and the level of co-operation obtained in implementing the programme.

When we reported our findings to the Governor and staff at Riverdale the *initial* reaction of staff could only be described as indifferent. The vast majority indicated that they believed that bullying was endemic within prisons and in other ways of life such as schools and the armed forces.

No member of staff indicated they already knew about the precise nature and extent of bullying at Riverdale as described by the inmates we interviewed prior to our report to the Governor. A certain amount of hostility toward the authors occurred which seemed to be due to the fact that we were drawing attention to something that was rationalised as 'happening everywhere' and inter alia happened at Riverdale. We do not wish to indicate that this attitude had led to bullying at Riverdale being condoned by staff but it is a fact that the number of inmates being placed on report for bullying prior to our investigation had been very low. Following these initial reactions, staff became extremely concerned to combat the problem by suggesting ways of dealing with bullying. These were incorporated by the Governor in the preventative measures adopted in the anti-bullying package.

One specific objection which was raised by a number of individuals, to studying bullying per se, and hence dealing with the problem if it were found to exist at unacceptable levels in prisons, is of particular note in terms of the cost of preventative measures. It was asserted that if bullying is found to occur, this leads to demands for extra staff to deal with the problem, which are unrealistic at a time of economic restraint. The current study demonstrates that this assertion is false. Unrealistic demands were not made. Two prison auxiliaries were employed on patrol duties to free prison officers for other duties but neither management nor union asked for a dramatic increase in manning levels precisely because the problem could be and indeed was dealt with successfully by existing staff.

Finally, similar principles of 'crime prevention' which were applied at Riverdale can be applied in any institution suffering similar problems. Whether such disturbing bullying activities are occurring elsewhere is doubtful but this is an empirical question and can only be discovered by research. That bullying can be controlled to an acceptable degree is evidenced by the situationally focussed measures implemented by the Prison Department at Riverdale.

CHAPTER 14

Effective Action against Bullying – the Key Problems

David Thompson and Peter K Smith

A simple notion concealing complex causes

As can be readily understood from the opening chapter, bullying is a complex social problem with a range of different 'causes', all of which may be relevant in considering any particular instance. These causes can range from aspects of the current personality of the bullying individual, ably reviewed by Besag (1989), through the ways that person has learnt to influence or dominate the people in their immediate social groups, to the values expressed by institutional practices in the school or residential home and to particular points about the quality of supervision exercised by the adults or other people responsible for order.

The problem of bullying is in some senses deeply rooted in human experience, as it basically consists of the over-use of violence to establish social dominance, in ordinary interpersonal situations, and both violence and social dominance are likely to be continuing facets of experience in a complex society as they have been before this. Simple issues of social dominance in groups are also, of course, inter-linked with more complex issues of leadership in social groups, although studies of leadership indicate that the task to be done is a significant element in the way that the group chooses a leader for itself. In this way leadership as it occurs amongst adolescents and young adults is a much more complex social phenomenon than dominance, but clearly there is some relationship between them. It is likely therefore that bullying as a social activity is related to fairly basic aspects of the way children learn to be social. This needs to be recognised as such by those adults responsible for the proper support of children's learning and development, both parents and the other professionals involved in various social institutions.

What we have been saying about the deep-rooted aspects of some of the causes of bullying also, of course, refers to the way in which some children and some adolescents find themselves pushed into playing the role of victim in the emerging social patterns. Like the children who at present learn to behave in a bullying manner in social groups, so many victims enter social life as children with a lesser tendency to behave aggressively or even assertively and what seems to be a slightly greater difficulty in making effective social relationships with peers (Besag, 1989) and find that the patterns of social interaction leave them on the margins of groups, waiting to be 'picked on' by a child interested in demonstrating dominance at very little cost to themselves.

Some of the uncertainties and differences in the estimation of the extent of bullying also reflects the complexity of the causes and the variations in the perception of bullying by the different parties involved. At present, the definition of bullying adopted by the 'classical researcher' tends to be the one which originated in the early Scandinavian studies, that is where a number of children, usually boys, intimidate a lone victim, using certainly aggressive and often physically violent means. This includes minimal expectation on behalf of the aggressors of any material gain. However, talking to children, their perceptions easily shade over into including any situation involving unprovoked aggression, whether or not the odds are as uneven as described above. Talking to black children about their experience of bullying, it is clear that their definition can easily be extended even further to include fairly ritualised name calling with a heavily racist bias in the general 'bullying' category. When talking to children who occasionally bully other children, it is clear that their perceptions of the incident are far less specific and negative than are those of the victims – and the incident is defended as just a little bit of fun. The best estimate of the extent of bullying in a given situation then is liable to be at least partially dependent on the perceptions and definitions accepted by the persons in that situation. The extent of bullying in a given group of children also seems to be related to the presence or absence inside that general group of specific highly active bullies, and as that group of bullies goes up the age ranges in a school the incidents of bullying can rise and fall in each year group as that group of particular individuals passes through. In spite of this general variation in individual perceptions there is a certain amount of agreement as to what actions can be described as bullying, as shown by Arora and Thompson (1987).

What to do about it – and where to start?

As can be seen from this book, what to do about bullying can include a wide variety of procedures, which may happen inside or outside the institution primarily involved with the children. The range of possible activities varies from simple administrative procedures such as amending the patterns of adult supervision of the places where bullying can occur, to fairly complex measures involving attempts to change the social climate of the particular institutions concerned, and to reflect this change in climate by adopting more or less complex new procedures to which all staff and most students are committed. This includes, of course, the various procedures to support the victims and change the behaviour of the bullies.

Administrative means of prevention

One of the frequently mentioned means of prevention of bullying is simply to increase the amount of supervision by adults and senior pupils in school of those areas where bullying is likely to occur. Identifying those areas which are relatively unsupervised at present is clearly a task for consultation with a number of staff and probably with the children as well. Places of course also includes times – even if places are as well supervised as classrooms generally are, if children can predict when a teacher will not be present, these regularities in teachers habits can be used to give a window of opportunity for the bullies and their support groups.

The two problems with such a tight supervision policy however, are (a) the sheer number of staff available for supervision activities, and (b) the maintenance of a system after it has been established. The problem of insufficient staff for supervision can be helped to some extent by extending a prefect system, especially where those duties are interpreted as 'befriending' groups of younger children as well as the more usual control aspects. This can work well when the children in the first year of a secondary school can have their main teaching class-rooms altogether in the main part of the school. This gives an area where the presence of older children can be easily identified, and also an area where the prefects can be involved in a general supervisory capacity. With care, this can also be an area which is generally available for children during breaks and lunchtimes, to give a base for children who feel themselves vulnerable in the general school environment. Systems of this nature also make it easier for temporary or transitory adult staff to supervise the unstructured times, for example, people involved with lunchtime supervision.

The second issue, that of maintenance of a supervision system, requires the same kind of bureaucratic control as any other school system does. Clear specification of which staff and students are responsible for what areas, good timing, and methods for staff and prefects to bring up flaws in the system all help to give everyone a feeling that the maintenance of an effective supervision system is important. The simpler and clearer a system, the easier it is for new staff to learn how to take part in it.

The necessary attitude changes amongst staff and students

The bulk of anti-bullying work, as can be seen from this book and other works in the field, deals with initiating and spreading such attitude changes, pastoral and disciplinary procedures, and also spreading those aspects of personal, social and moral education which define a set of values antagonistic to bullying. This then makes it possible to create social expectations of behaviours and procedures which reduce bullying.

How then can such social attitudes be created? When free expression is possible and accepted, most children clearly hold these attitudes already – they would far rather that bullying did not occur – and prefer to organise their social communications in a way which minimises hurtful aggression and violence. As argued elsewhere, however, staffs of many institutions tend to feel that a certain amount of bullying is inevitable and learning how to deal successfully with it can almost be seen as one of the stages of growing up. This approach of course conveniently minimises the responsibility of the adults to do anything about it themselves. One of the common ways in which adults become more aware of the importance of the issue in their own schools is when a survey of incidence is completed, and it is clear from the results that bullying is much more widespread and causing appreciably more distress than had been anticipated. Because of its awareness-raising functions, it is important that as many of the staff of the institutions as possible are associated with the completion of that survey work and discussion of its findings.

Even at this level though, concerns of staff to deal with bullying specifically are unlikely to have much emotional energy and momentum for change unless they are expressed in the general context of a responsibility for pastoral care of the children, which stresses children's welfare generally as an important aspect of the primary task of the particular institution. It is likely that most institutions dealing with children and young people have some existing system for managing general welfare issues, which can provide a nucleus of staff and experience while supporting and maintaining any institutional changes.

A further group of people who are, of course, extremely concerned by bullying are parents. They are often very concerned, but equally often lack any but the most obvious strategies for communicating to the children about bullying. With active support from the school however, parents can provide a significant source of emotional energy and even social sanctions in the struggle to develop an anti-bullying culture and deal satisfactorily with specific bullying incidents.

Supporting the 'silent majority'

Most children and young people do not approve of bullying where it involves hurt, but in the absence of clear institutional norms and procedures usually tolerate it when it occurs, recognising its enclosed nature as a predictable part of the interaction between their peers. However one of the real functions of schools is to socialise children into acceptable adult patterns of behaviour, including the idea to minimise aggression and violence as a means of ordering social relationships. After this point, people of different political complexions would then tend to either substitute a stress on the values of cooperation and mutual support, or task related competition, but both would agree on the importance of minimizing aggression and violence.

We have seen examples in this volume of ways in which this can be worked towards in school. These include simple statements of the aims and goals of the institution, often at a bureaucratic level in presentation material; the expression of these norms and values in personal and social education curriculum; educational activities, usually in the humanities subjects, stressing emotional identifications with the victims; and structured methods of skilled training through group work. One of the key aspects of these processes is the whole issue of bullying across an ethnic divide – where the usual bullying process strays into racial harassment and racism itself. For children and staff in multiracial schools, this aspect is never far from the surface.

One of the dilemmas of a 'cooperation and support' set of social norms is that it can clash with the common 'discipline' procedures. These usually involve a certain amount of 'institutional aggression' expressed and carried through by the adults in the community, in an attempt to achieve sanctions which act as punishments for the crime. Some workers would argue strongly that disciplinary processes of this nature, when used in dealing with obvious incidents of bullying, tend to weaken the very social norms which the general preventative effort is being directed to. They would support the use of discussions involving the bullies, the victims, the bystanders, and significant staff, to demonstrate the emotional hurt to the victims and involve the bullies themselves in defining some restitution for the hurt. Pikas (1989) gives a useful discussion of this as a 'common concern' method. He summarises the dialogue during individual discussions with students involved in 'mobbing' as structured round 5 statements:

(1) I would like to talk to you because I've heard you've been mean towards Jimmy.
(2) What do you know about it?
(3) All right, we've talked about it long enough.
(4) What should we do now? What do you suggest?
(5) That's good. We shall meet together in a week then you can tell me how you've been getting on.

As used by Pikas, the talks initially involve the children in the 'bullying' group, and subsequently the victim. Later group talks may or may not include the victim, depending on circumstances.

Barriers to progress

Given the clarity of the procedures such as described earlier in this volume and the measures of success achieved by these procedures through various informal and formal evaluation methods, why does it often feel so difficult to bite the bullet and begin to implement such procedures? There are of course many emotions which make individuals and institutions draw back. Some of these are natural and are the usual ones expected in launching any process of organizational change

– the uncertainty as to whether all the efforts will have a pay-off, and the size of that pay-off; the staff development issues in constructing a group consensus and sufficient skills in enough individual members of staff to carry through changes of this nature; and particularly at present in almost all publicly funded institutions, the morale sapping pressures of other work, under-resourcing and lack of public recognition. All these apply just as much when considering educationally and socially valid innovations such as the ones described here as they do when contemplating the latest set of budgetary control regulations.

Given a finite amount of human energy, institutions have to make their choices as to current priorities. On the other hand, a certain amount of energy and time will be already expended in dealing with the results of bullying activities; and as many other anti-bullying procedures also support more traditional school values and activities such as personal and social education, parent involvement, and an effective pastoral care process, it could be argued that the adoption of a specific anti-bullying set of strategies in as many aspects of school life as possible would in fact serve to maintain and strengthen these existing aspects of school life by giving them a specific focus for a period of time. To use an all-too-common management phrase, the period of introduction of an anti-bullying set of strategies could be seen as an opportunity not as a problem.

However, some of the justifiable hesitations are undoubtedly related to the emotional sensitivity of the problem and its solutions. The first thought in the heads of many staff members will be the risk of 'going public on bullying'. If the school suddenly sets up a visible anti-bullying strategy, is this an admission that the school has got a problem? Will the local press get hold of the issue? Will enrolment suffer as a result? Much of the work on parent attitudes and junior school children's attitudes to secondary schools seem to indicate that there is a near universal perception that bullying goes on in schools anyway. This view is even shared by the schools staff – the issue is the parents and children see it as being very significant whereas the staff often are quite honestly persuaded that it is of very little significance in the overall life of the school.

'Going public' may in fact only appear as at last listening to the parental concerns which existed already, rather than admitting a problem exists where none did before, and the public recognition by the school could be presented as an important strengthening of the pastoral discipline systems to reduce a problem which is known to exist to some extent in all schools anyway. The more the general issue is highlighted in the national press, the less easy will schools find it to make the claim, 'It doesn't happen in this school', and be believed. The statement will be much more credible if it is linked to widely known and specific procedures to minimise bullying. At one school which had instituted such procedures for the preceding four years, one research study found that a random sample of 4th year boys universally denied that there was any bullying in their year group – giving greatly enhanced credibility to the school's policies, procedures and managerial efficiency (Thompson and Arora, 1991).

A further inhibitor specific to anti-bullying strategies is that a reasonably large number of staff, including at least a proportion of the very senior staff must feel relatively relaxed when dealing with children's real emotional concerns, and with parent's real emotional concerns. To do this, this must themselves feel relatively confident in their abilities to deal satisfactorily with strong emotions, and to have had sufficient training of whatever sort to have some idea what a satisfactory outcome might be, and the stages by which this may be achieved. Whilst these abilities are undoubtedly present in some members of staff of almost every institution dealing with children, they are certainly not present in all members of staff in such institutions. Schools, colleges and children's homes do have need for people skilled in budgetary control, the organisation of the curriculum, and information technology as well as those whose strengths are in dealing with emotional relationships, and staff members with skills across all these areas are indeed worth their weight in gold.

The two general sets of people skills needed for an effective anti-bullying strategy are firstly, that which can be described as youth work or group work skills. This means that the staff member is used to handling groups of young people when the curriculum and the methods of teaching are very child-centred, and the teacher's role tends to that of a first among equals rather than a fount of all wisdom. If the silent majority is to be involved at all in the creation and maintenance of anti-bullying norms and values, they have to be approached through this style of work. A second style of work which again is sometimes necessary, or could be said to be necessary for only a minority of staff, is that of the counsellor. This would mean dealing (probably individually) with children, their anxieties and distresses and painful emotional reactions, in a way which allowed the children full expression of feelings, would help them see that others shared their concerns, and would help to find ways of improving the situation. This counselling role would also include the skills of dealing with parents' emotional reactions in the same way, and of knowing the ways in which such emotional reactions can be stabilised and used to support positive action to solve this specific problem.

Some members of staff of most institutions either would have or could be quite capable of developing such skills to form this level of resource for the school, but many members of staff would want to avoid this degree of emotional involvement with individual children and would see their greatest contributions to the school being elsewhere. It is likely that people with either or both of these sets of skills would be found in association with a pastoral care system, through the usual processes of mutual selection which operates between individuals and their occupational niches. However, it may be necessary for a senior management wishing to introduce specific anti-bullying strategies across the school to consider the levels of interest and skill of their pastoral care staff and of others in significant positions in the school, and to take whatever staff development activities are necessary to increase and support those skills. This may involve school staff development procedures inside the school organisation, such as pairing of experienced and inexperienced staff together when involved with group work or counselling activities, or specific out-of-school training activities for certain staff members.

This leads onto the third specific issue to be considered when adopting anti-bullying strategies, how best to involve outside agencies and their skills in the procedures being set up in school. We have examples in this book of outside theatre groups being used to support personal and social educational activities, of educational psychologists working jointly with school staff in group work, and of research workers being involved with the assessment and monitoring procedures alongside school staff. Such individuals from such agencies can bring specific skills into the school which can greatly strengthen the schools' ability to develop certain aspects of its own practice, but all the issues of successfully working together remain – the establishment of roles and relationships, the explicit adoption of common value systems, and possibly most important of all, the explicit definition of roles of the outsiders in such a way that they are perceived as supportive by the rest of the school staff. In the last resort, the bullying problem remains a part of the social interplay which takes place between young people, their peer groups, their teachers and their parents, and to achieve a successful minimisation of the problem it is this community which has to recognise its ownership of the problem, and its achievements in tackling it.

References

Ahmad, Y, and Smith, P. K. (1990) 'Behavioural measures: bullying in schools'. *Newsletter of Association for Child Psychology and Psychiatry*, **12**, 26–27.

Arora, C. M. J. (1989) 'Bullying – action and intervention'. *Pastoral Care in Education*, **7**, 44–47.

Arora, C. M. J. and Thompson, D. A. (1987) 'Defining bullying for a secondary school'. *Education and Child Psychology*, **4**, 110–120.

Battle, J. (1981) *Culture-free Self-esteem Inventories for Children and Adults*. Seattle: Special Child Publications.

Besag, V. (1989) *Bullies and Victims in Schools*. Milton Keynes: Open University Press.

Bjorkqvist, K., Ekman, K. and Lagerspetz, K. (1982) 'Bullies and victims: their ego picture, ideal ego picture and normative ego picture'. *Scandinavian Journal of Psychology*, **23**, 307–313.

Blatchford, P. (1989) *Playtime in the Primary School: Problems and Improvements*. Windsor: NFER-Nelson.

Brier, J. M. (1988) 'Developing a structural social development programme in an inner city school'. In P. Lang (ed), *Thinking About . . . Personal and Social Education in the Primary School*. Oxford: Basil Blackwell.

Burnage Report (1989) *Murder in the Playground*. London: Longsight Press.

Clarke, R. G. V. (1983) 'Situational crime prevention'. In M. Tonry and N. Morris (eds), *Crime and Justice: An Annual Review of Research*. Chicago: University of Chicago Press.

Cowie, H. and Rudduck, J. (1988, 1991) *Learning Together, Working Together*, Vol.1: *Co-operative Group Work: An Overview*; Vol.2: *School and Classroom Studies*; Vol.3: *Co-operative Learning: Traditions and Transitions*; Vol.4: *Co-operative Group Work in the Multi-ethnic Classroom*. BP Educational Service, P.O. Box 30, Blacknest, Alton, Hampshire GU34 4PX.

Dodge, K. A. and Frame, C. L. (1982) 'Social cognitive biases and deficits in aggressive boys'. *Child Development*, **53**, 620–635.

Dodge, K. A., Pettit, G. S., McClaskey, C. L. and Brown, M. M. (1986) 'Social competence in children'. *Monographs of the Society for Research in Child Development*, **51**(2), 1–85.

Dryden, W. (1989) *Rational-emotive Counselling in Action*. London: Sage Publications.

Dunning, E., Murphy, P. and Williams, J. (1988) *The Roots of Football Hooliganism: An Historical and Sociological Study*. London: Routledge & Kegan Paul.

Elliott, M. (1986) *Kidscape Training Pack: for Use with Primary Children*. London: Kidscape.

Elliott, M. (ed) (1991) *Bullying: A Practical Guide to Coping for Schools*. Harlow: Longman.

Elton Report (1989) *Discipline in Schools*. London: HMSO.

Feld, B. C. (1977) *Neutralising Inmate Violence: Juvenile Offenders in Institutions.* Cambridge, Mass.: Ballinger.

Foster, P., Arora, C. M. J. and Thompson, D. A. (1990) 'A whole school approach to bullying'. *Pastoral Care in Education*, 8.

Garcia, I. F. and Perez, G. Q. (1989) 'Violence, bullying and counselling in the Iberian Peninsula: Spain'. In E. Roland and E. Munthe (eds), *Bullying: An International Perspective.* London: David Fulton.

Gilmartin, B. G. (1987) 'Peer group antecedents of severe love-shyness in males'. *Journal of Personality*, 55, 467–489.

Guerra, N. G. and Slaby, R. G. (1989) 'Evaluative factors in social problem solving by aggressive boys'. *Journal of Abnormal Child Psychology*, 17, 277–289.

Hall, J. and Baker, R. (1973) 'Token economy systems: breakdown and control'. *Behaviour Research and Therapy*, 11, 253–263.

Herbert, G. (1989) 'A whole-curriculum approach to bullying'. In D. P. Tattum and D. A. Lane (eds), *Bullying in Schools*. Stoke-on-Trent: Trentham Books.

Hopson, B. and Scally, M. (1980) *Life Skills Teaching Programmes, No 1.* Leeds: Life Skills Associates (Department of Education, Leeds University).

Judson, S. (ed) (1984) *A Manual on Non-violence and Children.* Philadelphia: New Society Publishers.

Kelly, E. and Cohn, T. (1988) *Racism in Schools: New Research Evidence.* Stoke-on-Trent: Trentham Books.

Kidscape, (1986a) *Bullying: a Pilot Study*; (1986b) *Bully Courts.* Kidscape, 3rd floor, Europe House, World Trade Centre, London E1 9AA.

Lane, D. (1989) Violent histories: bullying and criminality. In D. P. Tattum and D. A. Lane (eds), *Bullying in Schools*. Stoke-on-Trent: Trentham Books.

Laslett, R. (1982) 'A children's court for bullies'. *Special Education*, 9, 9–11.

Lowenstein, L. F. (1978) 'Who is the bully?' *Bulletin of the British Psychological Society*, 31, 147–149.

Malik, G. (1990) *Bullying – an investigation of race and gender aspects.* Unpublished M.Sc. thesis, Department of Education, University of Sheffield.

Masheder, M. (1986) *Let's Co-operate.* Peace Education Project, 6 Endsleigh St., London WC1H 0DX.

McConnon, S. (1989) (a) *Self-esteem*; (b) *The Nature of Friendship*; (c) *The Skills of Friendship.* London: Macmillan.

Mellor, A. (1990) 'Bullying in Scottish secondary schools'. *Spotlights*, 23, Edinburgh: SCRE.

Munthe, E. (1989) 'Bullying in Scandinavia'. In E. Roland and E. Munthe (eds), *Bullying: An International Perspective.* London: David Fulton.

Neill, S. (1991) *Classroom Non-verbal Communication.* London: Routledge.

Newson, J. and Newson, E. (1984) 'Parents perspectives on children's behaviour in school'. In N. Frude and H. Gault (eds), *Disruptive Behaviour in Schools.* New York: Wiley.

Northumberland Education Department (1989) *Let's Get On – Improving Social Skills.* Psychological Services, Tyne House, Hepscott Park, Stannington, Morpeth, Northumberland.

O'Moore, A.M. and Hillery, B. (1989) 'Bullying in Dublin schools'. *Irish Journal of Psychology*, **10**, 426-441.

Olweus, D. (1978) *Aggression in the Schools: Bullies and Whipping Boys.* Washington, D.C.: Hemisphere.

Olweus, D. (1979) 'Stability of aggressive reaction patterns in males: A review'. *Psychological Bulletin*, **86**, 852-875.

Olweus, D. (1989) 'Bully/victim problems among schoolchildren: basic facts and effects of a school based intervention program'. In K. Rubin and D. Pepler (eds), *The Development and Treatment of Childhood Aggression.* Hillsdale, N.J.: Erlbaum.

Parker, J.G. and Asher, S.R. (1987) 'Peer relations and later personal adjustment: are low-accepted children at risk?' *Psychological Bulletin*, **102**, 357-389.

Patterson, G.R., DeBaryshe, D. and Ramsey, E. (1989) 'A developmental perspective on antisocial behaviour'. *American Psychologist*, **44**, 329-335.

Pavey, J. (1990) 'Bullying: how serious a problem?' *Crime Prevention News*, Jan-March, 11-14.

Pawluk, C.J. (1989) 'Social construction of teasing'. *Journal for the Theory of Social Behaviour*, **19**, 145-167.

Perry, D.G., Kusel, S.J. and Perry, L.C. (1988) 'Victims of peer aggression'. *Developmental Psychology*, **24**, 807-814.

Pikas, A. (1989) 'A pure concept of mobbing gives the best results for treatment'. *School Psychology International*, **10**, 95-104.

Polsky, H. (1962) *Cottage 6.* New York: Wiley.

Price, J.M. and Dodge, K.A. (1989) 'Reactive and proactive aggression in childhood: relations to peer status and social context dimensions'. *Journal of Abnormal Child Psychology*, **17**, 455-471.

Remocker, A.J. and Storch, E.T. (1987) *Action Speaks Louder: Handbook of Non-verbal Group Techniques.* Harlow: Longman.

Roland, E. (1989) 'Bullying: the Scandinavian research tradition'. In D.P. Tattum and D.A. Lane (eds), *Bullying in Schools.* Stoke-on-Trent: Trentham Books.

Roland, E. and Munthe, E. (eds) (1989) *Bullying: An International Perspective.* London: David Fulton.

Rutter, M., Maughan, B., Mortimore, P. and Ouston, J. (1979) *Fifteen Thousand Hours.* Shepton Mallet: Open Books.

Saunders, A. and Remsberg, B. (1986) *The Stress-proof Child.* New York: New American Library.

Smith, P.K. (1991) 'The silent nightmare: bullying and victimisation in school peer groups'. *The Psychologist*, **4**.

Smith, P.K. and Boulton, M.J. (1990) 'Rough-and-tumble play, aggression and dominance: perception and behaviour in children's encounters'. *Human Development*, **33**, 271-282.

Spence, S. (1977) *Social Skills Training with Children and Adolescents: A Trainer's Manual.* Windsor: NFER.

Stephenson, P. and Smith, D. (1989) 'Bullying in the junior school'. In D.P. Tattum and D.A. Lane (eds), *Bullying in Schools.* Stoke-on-Trent: Trentham Books.

Tattum, D. P. and Herbert, G. (1990) *Bullying – A Positive Response*. Faculty of Education, South Glamorgan Institute of Higher Education, Cyncoed Road, Cardiff CF2 6XD.

Tattum, D. P. and Lane, D. A. (1989) *Bullying in Schools*. Stoke-on-Trent: Trentham Books.

Thompson, D. A. and Arora, C. M. J. (1991) 'Pupils' views of the evidence of the effectiveness of a whole school policy to minimise bullying'. *Pastoral Care in Education*.

Tizard, B., Blatchford, P., Burke, J., Farquhar, C. and Plewis, I. (1988) *Young Children at School in the Inner City*. Hove: Lawrence Erlbaum Associates.

Yates, C. and Smith, P. K. (1989) 'Bullying in two English comprehensive schools'. In E. Roland and E. Munthe (eds), *Bullying: An International Perspective*. London: David Fulton.

Index

Caerleon
Library